The **Dyscalculia**
Resource Book

The **Dyscalculia** Resource Book

Games and Puzzles for ages 7 to 14

Ronit Bird

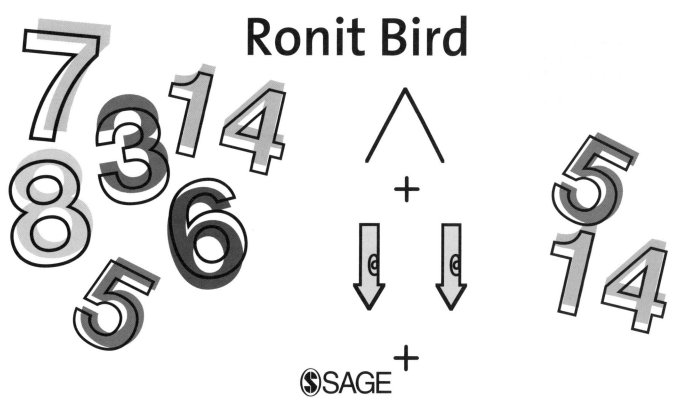

⑤SAGE

Los Angeles | London | New Delhi
Singapore | Washington DC

SAGE Publications Ltd
1 Oliver's Yard
55 City Road
London EC1Y 1SP

SAGE Publications Inc.
2455 Teller Road
Thousand Oaks, California 91320

SAGE Publications India Pvt Ltd
B 1/I 1 Mohan Cooperative Industrial Area
Mathura Road
New Delhi 110 044

SAGE Publications Asia-Pacific Pte Ltd
3 Church Street
#10-04 Samsung Hub
Singapore 049483

Library of Congress Control Number: 2010941387

British Library Cataloguing in Publication data

A catalogue record for this book is available from the British Library

ISBN 978-1-4462-0167-1
ISBN 978-1-4462-0168-8 (pbk)

FSC
www.fsc.org
MIX
Paper from
responsible sources
FSC® C013604

Typeset by C&M Digitals (P) Ltd, Chennai, India
Printed and bound by CPI Group (UK) Ltd, Croydon, CR0 4YY
Printed on paper from sustainable resources

Contents

Praise for this Book

'Ronit Bird is an extraordinary teacher with a lifetime of experience teaching dyscalculic children the basic principles of arithmetic. Here she makes this experience available to teachers and parents in a clear and systematic way. She provides a wealth of activities and games that will engage and stimulate the learner, and that rarely need more than paper, pencil and dice. Most importantly, she explains the learning goal of each exercise, and provides notes to the teacher about what to look for, and what to avoid. This book will make dyscalculics and their teachers happy.'

Professor Brian Butterworth, Institute of Cognitive Neuroscience, UCL

About the Author

Ronit Bird is a teacher whose interest in pupils with specific learning difficulties began with a focus on dyslexia. She qualified as a teacher at London University and subsequently gained a further qualification as a specialist teacher. While working with dyslexic pupils in a mainstream school, Ronit started to develop strategies and teaching activities to help support the learning of pupils who were experiencing difficulties in maths.

Ronit has taught in both primary and secondary settings, and has worked as a SENCO in both the independent and state sectors. Ronit also ran training courses on dyscalculia for Harrow subject leaders, teachers and teaching assistants as part of the Harrow Dyscalculia Project, working in an advisory capacity with the participating schools. She currently works as a teacher and as a contributor to professional development courses.

Ronit can be contacted through her website www.ronitbird.com where you will also find a list of Top Ten Tips for Parents and a forum through which you can discuss problems or suggestions with others who are interested in dyscalculia.

⊙ **Contents of CD** ⊙

Introduction

This book is for dyscalculic learners and those who teach and support them.

Children with specific maths difficulties have fundamental gaps in their understanding of basic numeracy that often stem from a hazy or faulty concept of the number system. So, in my work with dyscalculic pupils, I am always looking for ways to help them build up a sound mathematical understanding of numbers and their relationships. My approach, as I explain in *The Dyscalculia Toolkit* and *Overcoming Difficulties with Number*, is to concentrate on numeracy and arithmetic, starting with a variety of versatile concrete materials to provide practical experience and visual models, before moving gradually but steadily towards the more abstract and symbolic methods associated with higher level mathematics.

In common with other teachers working with learners who struggle with numeracy, I find that it is never enough to teach a topic just once or twice, no matter how well I manage to present the ideas or how keen my pupils are to learn. Repetition is the key, as is carefully planned progression in the tiniest of incremental steps, so that every new fragment of understanding rests on the solid foundation of what has already been learned and internalised. But, while practice is essential, straightforward duplication can be painfully dull and demotivating. This means that I have had to learn to be inventive about finding new and different ways of approaching each topic, so as to engage my pupils' interest as they explore and practise the mathematical ideas they are trying to master.

It is difficult to get pupils to practise productively between lessons. The concrete mathematical resources that are at the heart of my teaching methods are rarely to be found outside the maths classroom, and parents and teaching assistants are not always sure what kinds of activities are best for children who struggle with numeracy. At the same time, setting homework can be a real challenge for teachers because it is the mathematical processes that need practising, i.e. the methods and patterns of thought that lead to efficient calculation strategies, not the solutions themselves. A further challenge is to find enough material at the right level without overwhelming learners by using resources in which there is too rapid a progression of difficulty, or insulting them by presenting resources that are obviously aimed at much younger children.

These considerations have led me to create or adapt the games and puzzles in this book and to want to share them with anyone trying to help pupils who struggle with basic numeracy concepts. You are welcome to contact me through my website (www.ronitbird.com) with any feedback about how your children or pupils respond to the ideas in this book. On the website you will also find a list of Top Ten Tips for Parents and a forum through which you can discuss problems or suggestions with others who are interested in dyscalculia.

Why is this book full of games and puzzles rather than worksheets?

I am not a great fan of worksheets. The only kind I use are invariably based on practical activities that I have already undertaken with an individual student during a previous teaching session, resulting in something that is tailor-made to target a particular aspect of a recently taught technique or strategy. I make sure to avoid the kind of worksheet that is full of static exercises for pupils to work through on their own. All too often, worksheets are about drill and repetition, about training one's memory, about producing automatic responses as quickly as possible, about recording numbers on paper while conforming to traditional notation, about focusing on how many answers are correct or incorrect. None of this helps develop mathematical thinking. A diet of worksheet exercises makes pupils believe that the whole subject of mathematics is tediously repetitive, irrelevant and dull. What is more, a reliance on worksheets can be positively damaging in that they often do little more than provide children with extra practice in exactly those unhelpful methods and immature strategies that are holding them back.

In compiling this book, my intention has been to produce something as far removed from a book full of worksheets as possible. I want children to engage with numbers on a practical level and to see maths as something stimulating and challenging, a dynamic and satisfying activity. I therefore use games and puzzles as an integral part of my teaching approach. Games and puzzles are fun. They are intrinsically motivating. They captivate and stimulate, encouraging children to become willing participants in their own learning.

A further compelling advantage of the games and puzzles in this book is that, unlike worksheets, they have the capacity to provide different learning experiences on different occasions. Every time one of these games is played, the players can find themselves in a different situation, depending on the throw of the dice, the shuffling of the cards, or the actions of their opponent. Each time one of my puzzles is attempted, a new starting place might be chosen, leading to alternative pathways towards the same solution. This results in a varied mixture of different, but related, mathematical challenges being presented each time the games and puzzles are revisited, which in turn contributes to more exciting, engaging, enjoyable – and therefore more memorable – learning experiences.

What kind of games and puzzles does this book contain?

Of the 100 activities in this book, half are games and half are puzzles. All are suitable for a wide range of ages, being presented very simply without the gaudy colours and cartoon characters that render so many numeracy resources unsuitable for older learners. Each game or puzzle has a very narrow focus in terms of the numeracy topic it targets. The first 50 games and puzzles target addition and subtraction of numbers up to 20, while the last 50 games and puzzles target multiplication tables and division facts up to 10 × 10. Within each of these limited ranges, the games and puzzles are arranged so that they become progressively more challenging.

Roughly half the games are played with one or more opponent, while the other half are solitaire games to be played alone. All the puzzles are intended for children to tackle on their own, at their own pace.

The games include a mixture of board games and card or dice games. Most are games that I have devised myself, together with a few others that I have adapted from popular games including some traditional card games.

No equipment is required beyond what can be found in an average home: dice, dominoes, counters, coins, tokens, playing cards, paper and pencil. Where slightly unusual dice are proposed, such as a 10-sided die, instructions are given on how to adapt the standard 6-sided dice if those are the only kind to hand. Where digit cards are called for, packs of cards can be created by photocopying, laminating and cutting out those provided in the Appendix and on the CD, or ordinary playing cards can be substituted. At the end of this introduction, an overview of the games and puzzles in this book sets out each activity's main teaching focus together with a list of the necessary equipment.

The puzzles that I devised for this book are based on the popular Su Doku numerical logic puzzles. I have adapted the format to create two series of puzzles, with the puzzles in each series being methodically graduated in difficulty: a series of 25 Component Su Doku puzzles to provide a wealth of practice in splitting and recombining small amounts in order to focus on addition, subtraction and missing number relationships for numbers up to 20; and a series of 25 MAD puzzles (the initials standing for 'multiplication and division') to provide a wealth of practice in times tables facts up to 10 × 10. Both series of puzzles also provide practice in logical thinking. I have ensured that none of them requires guesswork, or trial and error, for their solution.

How do resources designed for dyscalculic learners differ from other numeracy resources?

The most important consideration is that dyscalculic learners need to address the gaps in their understanding of basic numeracy concepts. Many pupils with specific difficulties in maths do not have a coherent mental model of the number system, resulting in them resorting to either guesswork or relying on mechanistic and immature strategies. The most common example of this is a tendency to count up or down in ones on fingers for all types of calculation, even the simplest kind. To eradicate the unhelpful habit of ones-based thinking that holds so many pupils back, children need plenty of experience of chunking, joining, partitioning and recombining amounts, using concrete materials at first, followed by unlimited opportunities to practise the components of all the numbers up to 10.

Pupils with specific maths difficulties rarely notice patterns or make spontaneous connections between numbers or groups of items, and so may not realise that the numbers between 1 and 10 are the basis for repeating patterns through every successive decade of our decimal number system. Such pupils need to be introduced carefully to the numbers between 10 and 20, once their understanding of the first ten numbers is absolutely secure, so that they can begin to see and internalise the logic of the pattern repetitions that will enable them to apply their growing understanding to larger numbers.

A classic difficulty for people who are dyslexic or dyscalculic is with multiplication tables. Learners may be unable to memorise the tables and, unless shown how to make sense of them, may not be able to use any of the facts in any meaningful way. When trying to learn tables by heart, children with specific maths difficulties find that a focus on one table very often disturbs and distorts what they tried previously to memorise about another table. So, pupils need to be helped to understand connections between related tables and between related tables facts, and encouraged to direct their efforts away from memorising and towards getting as much reasoning practice as possible in the process of deriving the harder multiplication facts from the easier, well-known facts.

Pupils who struggle with numeracy often have significant memory weaknesses. For pupils who cannot reliably memorise facts and procedures, a teaching approach that focuses on understanding and on logical reasoning is essential. Whatever the numeracy topic, practice in deriving new facts from known facts is likely to be much more helpful than doomed attempts to develop automatic responses to basic arithmetic calculations through drill and repetition.

What follows from the above is that, not only do resources for dyscalculic pupils need to be very tightly focused on a single new idea at any one time, teachers need also to amass a large quantity of materials that all target the same narrow range of foundation skills. Within the essential repetition and revision, there must be enough variety to keep the learner engaged. At the same time, there should be a planned progression in steady sequential steps, with each new idea carefully building on skills previously practised. It is important to keep to a very gradual rate of progression in steps that are so small that it is possible for learners to experience success at every stage.

Pupils who find maths difficult need to concentrate hard for extended periods of time before anything new can be absorbed. The last thing they need is to be burdened by extra requirements, such as being expected to draw upon facts from other maths topics or other school subjects, while they are still struggling to learn a particular numeracy idea or technique. Pupils with specific maths difficulties are also better off without the distraction of pages crammed and cluttered with too much writing or too many numbers, and by childish illustrations that highlight the fact that they are working at a level that is well behind their chronological age.

It is unreasonable to insist that underachieving pupils write down every fact or calculation using the correct formal mathematical notation. Pupils who are sensitive about making repeated mistakes benefit from more practical and oral work rather than written work and should be encouraged to use informal jotting methods that are more closely allied to their normal patterns of thought.

A further consideration is that visualisation is a crucial medium through which people learn to connect concrete experience with abstract thought. Therefore, resources that feature clear, easily visualised, diagrammatic representations of numeracy operations are those that best help dyscalculic pupils to practise and develop all-important visualisation skills.

Are the games and puzzles suitable for homework?

The whole issue of homework is problematic. On the one hand, having pupils work on their own between lessons can be enormously valuable in reinforcing and consolidating any new ideas that they have just been taught but that they have not yet had a chance to internalise. On the other hand, so many pupils who struggle do so because of ingrained misconceptions and inefficient strategies, so that there is a real danger that sending work home will result in children reinforcing bad habits.

This dilemma is one I have regularly faced throughout my years of teaching. I have frequently been asked by concerned and supportive parents of dyscalculic children to set homework for their child. But, while I share their desire to speed up the process of learning and to help their child catch up with classmates as soon as possible, I know from experience that the wrong kind of homework can do more harm than good. My ambivalence stems from the fact that my teaching always focuses on process – making connections, teasing out efficient strategies, learning and rehearsing reasoning routes – not on producing answers. I am very reluctant to send home the kind of work that might, for all I know, be done on a calculator, or – even worse – by the child falling back on the very strategies that I am battling so hard to replace.

Over the years, I have developed strong opinions about how I can best help pupils who struggle with numeracy, so much so that I have always felt the need to create, adapt and develop my own resources in order that the material I use with my students properly reflects my own convictions about content, teaching approach, learning strategies and rate of progression. I have, by now, assembled a large resource bank of games and puzzles that are designed specifically to target the techniques I am trying to reinforce, and no others. Although many of the ideas relate to explicit teaching activities (see *The Dyscalculia Toolkit* and *Overcoming Difficulties with Number*) many others are suitable as reinforcement activities, either at school or at home. Of this last group, only those games and puzzles that do not require too much in the way of adult supervision and nothing in the way of specialist equipment have found their way into these pages, precisely to enable the activities in this book to provide a useful bank of homework resources.

Are the games in this book teaching games or practice activities?

I would hate anyone to pick up this volume and assume, because the games and puzzles within are played with cards and dice or paper and pencil, that I advocate teaching numeracy in an abstract manner. I do not. My habitual method of teaching is to start concretely, making extensive use of mathematical apparatus such as Cuisenaire rods and base-10 blocks. Only at a later stage do I begin to introduce diagrams and visualisation techniques so as to effect a deliberate and explicit transition between concrete and abstract methods of working.

My books, *The Dyscalculia Toolkit* and *Overcoming Difficulties with Number*, describe my approach to numeracy teaching in great detail and provide practical suggestions for hands-on teaching activities that can be taken directly into the classroom. The games and exercises in this book are designed to follow on from and complement those activities, by providing opportunities for pupils to practise particular techniques and strategies that have already been comprehensively taught. The contents of this book can, of course, be used in conjunction with any textbook and any approach to numeracy teaching, but those who use this book alongside my previous two publications will see that I have created or adapted these games and puzzles to provide opportunities for children to practise and reinforce the particular methods and techniques that I believe best help pupils build a solid foundation of numerical understanding.

I find it useful to distinguish between teaching, which must come first, and practice, which is what reinforces what has already been taught. The distinction is sufficiently important to prompt me to insert reminders in the text from time to time to the effect that the practice activities are intended to reinforce, not to replace, teaching for understanding. In several cases, the games presented here are paper-and-pencil versions of games that can and, indeed, should be played with concrete mathematical equipment first. In this way, these games can accelerate the transition between concrete and diagrammatic representation, which is a necessary step before abstract and symbolic mastery can be achieved.

The games and puzzles in this book are not just activities that happen to include numbers. They are intended to provide real learning opportunities. They are specifically designed to target those narrow but crucial foundation topics that dyscalculic learners find so very difficult to master, such as adding or subtracting in chunks rather than on fingers, or understanding and using multiplication tables. Learners with specific maths difficulties should not be expected to memorise too many facts but should, instead, be taught reasoning routes to work out what they need from first principles, basing their logic on a deep understanding of the underlying mathematical concepts. Many of the games and puzzles in this book are preceded by short practice exercises during which players rehearse the facts and the patterns of thought that will be called upon during play. Many others are designed to give pupils practical experience in deriving new facts by reasoning logically from the small repertoire of facts that are already securely known.

For whom is this book written?

I imagine my target audience belonging to one of two groups: parents, or school staff who directly support pupils with specific maths learning difficulties.

An important group for whom this book is intended includes those parents who wish to support their child at home but who know less than they would like about maths as a subject, or about modern methods of teaching numeracy, or about how dyscalculia, dyslexia or dyspraxia affects their child's learning. Many of the ideas in this book began as ideas for homework assignments in recognition of the fact that it is always easier for a parent to engage a child in a game than to have to supervise the more traditional forms of after-school homework. And, as I mention above, well-designed games and puzzles can provide powerful learning experiences.

I hope that the book will also have considerable appeal for non-specialist members of staff such as teaching assistants and learning support assistants. TAs and LSAs are so often the ones who work directly with pupils needing extra support, yet many of them lack the kind of detailed background subject knowledge that they feel they need to do the job properly.

Anybody involved in running or resourcing maths clubs or catch-up and revision sessions, whether the participants have any specific maths learning difficulties or not, will find numerous suitable ideas in this book.

Other members of staff who might find this book useful are busy class teachers, maths teachers and maths subject leaders in both junior and secondary schools. Junior teachers tend not to be maths specialists and are expected to cover so many curriculum subjects that it is unrealistic to expect expertise in each one of those subjects. At the other extreme, mathematics teachers in secondary schools are usually people who have always found maths easy and who have studied maths to a very high level, which may mean that they have trouble understanding the precise nature of their underachieving pupils' difficulties.

All teachers looking for differentiated numeracy activities, while contending with large classes and limited preparation time, will, I hope, welcome the fact that this book offers so many tried-and-tested games and puzzles specifically targeted at pupils who find maths a struggle.

This book will be of special interest to SENCOs and special needs teachers as well as to dyslexia, dyspraxia and dyscalculia specialists. The book is a ready-made resource suitable for any age between roughly 7 and 14, providing a bank of practical ideas for which the progression has been carefully calibrated, presented cleanly and simply so as not to distract the younger learners or patronise the older ones.

The games and puzzles are all ready to use with a minimum of preparation or special equipment. All the actual games and puzzles can be printed off from the CD accompanying this book. I believe all my readers will welcome this clarity and ease of use.

How to use this book

The 100 games and puzzles in this book are arranged in two sections so that you can start at the beginning of either section and work through each of the activities in turn. The puzzles usually alternate with the games, the sequence in which the activities are presented providing for a slow but steady increase in difficulty. In other words, I have deliberately created variety by ensuring that no two consecutive tasks are the same, while constructing a progression in which later activities build on ideas that have been targeted previously. Of course, there is no compulsion to either follow the sequence or to start from the beginning. The overview tables at the end of this introduction list the main numeracy focus of each activity so that you can easily choose an alternative programme of activities or a faster rate of progression.

In every school, there should be a teacher who has responsibility for either delivering or coordinating the specialist support offered to any pupil with dyscalculia or other maths learning difficulties. If you are that teacher, you can use this book to find a suitable game or puzzle for an individual pupil and then delegate the reinforcement activity to another member of staff or to the parents of the child. Simply print off the page containing the game or puzzle from the CD accompanying this book, but make sure the adult who will actually supervise the session with the child also has an opportunity to read the left-hand page in the book that precedes each activity.

The first page of each double-page spread contains a summary of the teaching points that the game or puzzle is designed to target, together with a list of the equipment needed. You can use the list of teaching points both to help identify which activities might meet the current needs of individual pupils and to make links to curriculum targets or levels. The listed teaching points also act as a set of criteria against which you can judge – before choosing the activity – whether the game or puzzle is at the right level, and after the activity is undertaken whether the game or puzzle has been successful and whether the child is now ready to move on to a more challenging activity.

Most importantly, the first page contains notes for whoever is acting as the supervising adult, giving clear directions for how to maximise the learning opportunity. For example, unless specifically warned, you might not realise that the whole point of a particular game would be undermined if the child were allowed to use fingers for counting during play. I have been so very particular about including detailed notes for the supervising adult that I apologise in advance for the inevitable repetition that sometimes occurs.

You will find that the rate of progression between one activity and the next is so small that the child should need only a minimum amount of help or correction. If the child makes a mistake, you should give a gentle hint to help towards self-correction rather than supply the correct answer directly. For example, if during the course of playing a game the child says, '3 plus 5 is 7', you could say, 'But 3 plus 4 is 7, so 3 plus 5 must be . . . what?' or 'Try again' rather than say either 'That's wrong' or 'It's 8'.

The game or puzzle page often needs to be completed in writing. The amount of recording in writing has been carefully judged so as not to overwhelm the pupil and not to overshadow the enjoyment of the game. Sometimes the recording is intended to be a way for the child to learn about informal notation, while at other times its aim is to help pupils become familiar with standard mathematical notation; both of these support the vital transition stage between concrete and abstract methods of calculation. Occasionally, the recording is simply an incentive for the child to complete the work and a way for the teacher to ensure that the game has, in fact, been played. Some games include no written elements and therefore no need for the page to be handed back to the teacher; these can be retained by the pupil and collected together to create a small store of numeracy games that can be brought out and played again on future occasions, for example during school holidays.

Each game or puzzle in this book takes very little time to complete. I believe in applying the adage 'little and often' to most situations in which a learner is at the early stages. I have provided enough activities in this book to be able to offer pupils a new reinforcement opportunity after every two or three lessons, especially since most of the games can, and should, be played several times. I generally find that daily practice for 5 or 10 minutes at a time is far more beneficial than weekly practice for an hour or more.

Please bear in mind that the games and puzzles in this book are designed to give pupils practice in techniques and strategies that they have already been taught. It would be a great mistake to give pupils calculators or multiplication squares in conjunction with these resources (although both have their uses in other situations). If pupils cannot manage the addition or multiplication demanded by a game or puzzle, it is up to us, as teachers, to show them how it is done. Once pupils have been given the strategies they need to solve simple arithmetic problems independently, these games and puzzles are ideal for providing enjoyable opportunities to practise the newly learned techniques.

In summary

This book provides:

- 50 games and puzzles targeting addition and subtraction, specifically designed to help children overcome their unhelpful habit of counting in ones for every calculation.

▶ 50 games and puzzles targeting multiplication and division, specifically designed to help children understand multiplication tables and learn how to find multiplication and division facts they do not immediately know.

▶ An enjoyable way for children to practise the particular numeracy skills that commonly cause problems to those with specific maths difficulties.

▶ Games and puzzles that require nothing in the way of specialist equipment.

▶ Activities that are ready to use. The accompanying CD contains all 100 games and puzzles so that individual or multiple copies can be easily printed off.

▶ Games that are easy to set up, simple to learn and quick to play.

▶ Activities that are ideal for homework assignments, or out-of-class support sessions, to reinforce numeracy learning between maths lessons.

▶ Games and puzzles that focus very narrowly on only one arithmetic topic at a time, with no presupposition of extraneous knowledge of other topics or other subjects.

▶ A very gradual rate of progression in small but steady sequential steps, with each new idea carefully building on skills practised in previous games and puzzles.

▶ A way of helping pupils think about and prepare for the necessary transition between concrete and abstract methods.

▶ Clear and detailed information about the teaching points of each game or puzzle, making it easy for the teacher to choose which games to offer individual pupils.

▶ Clear instructions for the supervising adult about what to say and what to focus on during play, making it easy for parents and teaching assistants to provide a productive learning experience.

▶ Games that are non-repetitive (i.e. the opposite of providing worksheets for practice) so that each time they are played they present different challenges.

▶ A focus on active and thoughtful engagement, during which oral responses far outnumber any requirement for recording in writing.

▶ A focus on understanding numeracy concepts rather than on memorising answers.

▶ A way of providing explicit practice in deriving answers logically from known facts as a strategy to circumvent memory difficulties.

▶ A large resource bank (half the activities in this volume) of custom-made puzzles based on the popular Su Doku puzzles, carefully graduated in difficulty.

▶ A large resource bank (almost two-thirds of the activities in this volume) of puzzles and solitaire games that children can tackle on their own, without supervision and at their own pace.

▶ A resource bank of games that can be used or adapted for more than two players, ideal for maths clubs and group catch-up or revision sessions.

▶ A resource bank of ideas that can be used in class as differentiation activities.

▶ Ideas that are targeted at a wide age range, presented without the garish colours and cartoon characters that make so many resources unsuitable for older learners.

▶ A layout that presents everything the supervising adult needs to know on one page, leaving the relatively uncluttered facing page to be copied or printed off and given to the child.

Part I Overview Table

		Number of players			Numeracy topic	Equipment needed	Page No.
		1	2	3			
1	Components & Key Components [1–10]		✓		Build numbers 1–10	2 dice	2
2	Collect 5s		✓		Components of 5	2 dice, counters	4
3	Clear the Deck of 6s	✓			Components of 6	Digit cards	6
4	3-in-a-Line Dominoes		✓		Key components 1–10	A die	8
5	Dot Pattern Stickers Race		✓	✓	Key components 1–10	A die, stickers	10
6	Components & Key Components [5–10]		✓	✓	Addition/key facts 5–10	2 dice, coloured pencils	12
7	Regroup		✓		Partition numbers 1–10	3 dice	14
8	Twos & Threes		✓		Plus or minus 2 or 3	Digit cards	16
9	Component Su Doku Puzzle	✓			Add/subtract up to 9	Pencil, rubber	18
10	Spotlight on 7 and 8	✓			Components of 7 and 8	Digit cards	20
11	Component Su Doku Puzzle	✓			Add/subtract up to 9	Pencil, rubber	22
12	Odd or Even Domino Ladders		✓		Odd or even 1–10	Dominoes	24
13	Component Su Doku Puzzle	✓			Add/subtract up to 9	Pencil, rubber	26
14	Odds & Evens Circuit		✓		Odd or even 1–10	A die, 2 tokens	28
15	Component Su Doku Puzzle	✓			Add/subtract up to 9	Pencil, rubber	30
16	Clear the Deck of 9s	✓			Components of 9, etc.	Digit cards	32
17	Component Su Doku Puzzle	✓			Add/subtract up to 11	Pencil, rubber	34
18	Equation Solitaire	✓			Subtraction below 10	Coloured pencils	36
19	Component Su Doku Puzzle	✓			Add/subtract up to 11	Pencil, rubber	38
20	Cuisenaire Rods Wall Game		✓		Complements to 10	Coloured pencils	40
21	Component Su Doku Puzzle	✓			Add/subtract up to 11	Pencil, rubber	42
22	Triad Families		✓	✓	Add/subtract up to 10	Digit cards	44
23	Component Su Doku Puzzle	✓			Add/subtract up to 11	Pencil, rubber	46
24	Banking Tens		✓	✓	Complements to 10	Digit cards	48
25	Bridging Race		✓	✓	Bridging through 10	2 dice, pencil	50
26	Component Su Doku Puzzle	✓			Add/subtract up to 13	Pencil, rubber	52
27	Addition Card War		✓		Addition up to 12 or <20	Digit cards	54
28	Component Su Doku Puzzle	✓			Add/subtract up to 13	Pencil, rubber	56
29	Domino Bonus Game		✓		Addition up to 12	Dominoes	58
30	Component Su Doku Puzzle	✓			Add/subtract up to 13	Pencil, rubber	60
31	Difference Card War		✓		Subtraction below 10	Digit cards	62
32	Component Su Doku Puzzle	✓			Add/subtract up to 13	Pencil, rubber	64
33	Cover the Number [Shut the Box]		✓		Add/subtract up to 12	2 dice	66
34	Component Su Doku Puzzle	✓			Add/subtract up to 15	Pencil, rubber	68
35	Triad Card & Domino Families		✓		Add/subtract up to 12	Digit cards, dominoes	70
36	Component Su Doku Puzzle	✓			Add/subtract up to 15	Pencil, rubber	72
37	Prisoners	✓			Components of 11, 12, 13	Playing cards	74
38	Component Su Doku Puzzle	✓			Add/subtract up to 15	Pencil, rubber	76
39	Cuisenaire Rods Staircase to 20		✓		Complements to 20	A die, coloured pencils	78
40	Component Su Doku Puzzle	✓			Add/subtract up to 15	Pencil, rubber	80
41	Component Su Doku Puzzle	✓			Add/subtract up to 11	Pencil, rubber	82
42	Component Su Doku Puzzle	✓			Add/subtract up to 17	Pencil, rubber	84
43	Difference Su Doku Puzzle	✓			Subtraction as difference	Pencil, rubber	86
44	Component Su Doku Puzzle	✓			Add/subtract up to 17	Pencil, rubber	88
45	Component Su Doku Puzzle	✓			Add/subtract up to 13	Pencil, rubber	90
46	Component Su Doku Puzzle	✓			Add/subtract up to 17	Pencil, rubber	92
47	Difference Su Doku Puzzle	✓			Subtraction as difference	Pencil, rubber	94
48	Component Su Doku Puzzle	✓			Add/subtract up to 17	Pencil, rubber	96
49	Component Su Doku Puzzle	✓			Add/subtract up to 17	Pencil, rubber	98
50	Standing Aces	✓			Addition up to 20	Playing cards	100

Part II Overview Table

	Number of players			Numeracy topic	Equipment needed	Page No.
	1	**2**	**3**			
51 Double & Half Dominoes		✓		Double/half 2–10	1–6 spot die	104
52 Cuisenaire Rods Pyramid		✓		Double/half 2–10	Coloured pencils	106
53 Butterfly Doubles [1–6]		✓		Double/half 1–12	1–6 die	108
54 Halving Odd Multiples of Ten	✓			Halve round numbers	6-sided die	110
55 MAD Puzzles	✓			Mult/div up to 4 × 4	Pencil, rubber	112
56 The 2 & 4 Times Tables Race		✓		2× and 4× tables	2 1–6 dice, counters	114
57 Five is Half of Ten		✓		5× and 10× tables	1–10 die (or 2 1–6 dice)	116
58 The 3× Table Coin Solitaire	✓			3× table	10 coins, stickers	118
59 MAD Puzzles	✓			Mult/div up to 5 × 5	Pencil, rubber	120
60 Key Multiples Bingo		✓		Key facts: 2×, 5×, 10×	1–10 die (or 2 1–6 dice)	122
61 MAD Puzzle	✓			Mult/div up to 5 × 5	Pencil, rubber	124
62 9s All-in-a-Row [9 is one less than 10]		✓		9× table	1–10 die (or 2 1–6 dice)	126
63 MAD Puzzle	✓			Mult/div up to 5 × 5	Pencil, rubber	128
64 The 9× Table Coin Solitaire	✓			9× table	10 coins, stickers	130
65 MAD Puzzle	✓			Mult/div up to 5 × 5	Pencil, rubber	132
66 Don't Walk if You Can Take the Bus!		✓		3× and 6× tables	1–10 die, pawn, 20 coins	134
67 MAD Puzzle	✓			Mult/div up to 6 × 6	Pencil, rubber	136
68 The 6× Table Coin Solitaire	✓			6× table	10 coins, stickers	138
69 MAD Puzzle	✓			Mult/div up to 6 × 6	Pencil, rubber	140
70 The 3× & 6× Tables Race		✓		3× and 6× tables	2 1–6 dice, counters	142
71 MAD Puzzle	✓			Mult/div up to 6 × 6	Pencil, rubber	144
72 Butterfly Doubles [7–9]		✓		Double 7, 8 and 9	6-sided die	146
73 MAD Puzzle	✓			Mult/div up to 6 × 6	Pencil, rubber	148
74 Tables on a Number Line		✓		6×, 7× and 8× tables	1–3 die (or 6-sided die)	150
75 MAD Puzzle	✓			Mult/div up to 6 × 6	Pencil, rubber	152
76 The 7× Table Coin Solitaire	✓			7× table	10 coins, stickers	154
77 MAD Puzzle	✓			Mult/div up to 7 × 7	Pencil, rubber	156
78 Compete for Harder Facts of 7× Table		✓		6 × 7 to 9 × 7	6-sided die, pencil	158
79 MAD Puzzle	✓			Mult/div up to 7 × 7	Pencil, rubber	160
80 Advanced Doubling & Halving Track		✓	✓	Double/halve 2-digit nos.	1–6 die, 2 or 3 tokens	162
81 MAD Puzzle	✓			Mult/div up to 7 × 7	Pencil, rubber	164
82 The 8× Table Coin Solitaire	✓			8× table	10 coins, stickers	166
83 MAD Puzzle	✓			Mult/div up to 7 × 7	Pencil, rubber	168
84 Compete for Harder Facts of 8× Table		✓		6 × 8 to 9 × 8	6-sided die, pencil	170
85 MAD Puzzle	✓			Mult/div up to 7 × 7	Pencil, rubber	172
86 The 4 & 8 Times Tables Race		✓		4× and 8× tables	2 1–6 dice, counters	174
87 MAD Puzzle	✓			Mult/div up to 8 × 8	Pencil, rubber	176
88 Top of the Tables Square		✓		6 × 6 to 9 × 9	2 6-sided die	178
89 MAD Puzzle	✓			Mult/div up to 8 × 8	Pencil, rubber	180
90 Areas on a Grid		✓	✓	Multiplication as area	6-sided die, pencils	182
91 MAD Puzzle	✓			Mult/div up to 8 × 8	Pencil, rubber	184
92 MAD Puzzle	✓			Mult/div up to 8 × 8	Pencil, rubber	186
93 Factors Track Race		✓		Factors	2 tokens, coin, pencil	188
94 MAD Puzzle	✓			Mult/div up to 8 × 8	Pencil, rubber	190
95 MAD Puzzle	✓			Mult/div up to 8 × 8	Pencil, rubber	192
96 MAD Puzzle	✓			Mult/div up to 8 × 8	Pencil, rubber	194
97 MAD Puzzle	✓			Mult/div up to 8 × 8	Pencil, rubber	196
98 MAD Puzzle	✓			Mult/div up to 9 × 9	Pencil, rubber	198
99 MAD Puzzle	✓			Mult/div up to 9 × 9	Pencil, rubber	200
100 R for Remainder		✓	✓	Remainders in division	3 1–6 dice, tokens	202

PART I

Addition and Subtraction Games and Puzzles

1 Components & Key Components [1–10] – a game for 2 players

Teaching points

▶ The key components of all the numbers up to 10. The words 'key components' here refer to the doubles and near-doubles facts, e.g. 5 and 4 are the key components of 9.

▶ Practice in recognising the dice patterns.

▶ Only the numbers 1 to 5 (but not 6) are key components of the numbers up to 10.

▶ The same small number can be one of the key components of up to three larger numbers. For example, the number 4 is one of the key components of 7 and of 8 and of 9.

▶ Any number can be built by combining two smaller quantities (the basis of addition).

▶ Any number can be partitioned into two smaller components (the basis of subtraction).

Note to member of staff or parent

▶ Make sure the child is learning to recognise the dice patterns, not counting the dice spots.

▶ The child is not allowed to add by counting in ones, on fingers or otherwise. Anyone who is not yet at this stage should spend more time learning through concrete materials.

▶ Explain to the child that 'key facts' are so called because they are important facts that unlock a logical route to other, related facts. A focus on key facts, e.g. learning a single fact for each number up to 10, means minimising the number of facts that have to be committed to memory.

▶ Make sure the child understands what is meant by 'key components'. For example, 5 and 4 are the key components of 9 because 5 + 4 is a near-doubles fact. Other components of 9 are 3 and 6, or 2 and 7, or 8 and 1, but these facts are not key facts.

▶ Point out to the child that the colouring task is a way of highlighting the most important combinations, i.e. the key component facts, not simply a way of scoring this game.

▶ Once both players have had nine turns each to throw the dice and draw the dominoes, it is the child who should undertake the scoring by finding, colouring and reading aloud the key facts on both players' boards.

▶ The game should be played more than once and on more than one occasion.

Equipment needed

Two ordinary 6-sided spot dice. A second game board for an opponent. A pencil each and two coloured pencils in two different colours.

1. Components & Key Components [1–10]

Name:

Date:

When to hand it in:

Instructions

Take turns to throw two dice and throw again if you get a 6. Copy the two dot patterns from the dice onto any domino shape on your board, drawing each dice pattern separately on either side of the same domino. Announce (but do not record in digits) each number as you copy it as well as the total value of the domino that is created, i.e. the sum of the two dice.

When each player's game board is full, use a coloured pencil to shade in all the dominoes with a doubles pattern, for instance an 8 that is built of two 4s.

This is a key fact which must be read aloud: say "The key fact about 8 is double 4" or "4 and 4 are the key components of 8".

Use a different colour to shade in any dominoes with near-doubles facts, such as 4 and 3, 4 and 5, etc. Say these key facts aloud, too, like this: "The key components of 7 are 3 and 4".

The winner is the player with the most dominoes showing key component facts.

Components & Key Components [1–10]

Player 1

2   Collect 5s – a game for 2 players

Teaching points

▶ There are only two ways of building the number 5 from two components.

▶ Inside the pattern of 5 one can see the pattern of 3 superimposed onto the pattern of 2.

▶ Inside the pattern of 5 one can see the pattern of 1 superimposed onto the pattern of 4.

▶ The commutativity of addition, i.e. 4 + 1 is the same as 1 + 4, and 2 + 3 = 3 + 2.

▶ Mental addition of two numbers below 5 to create a total of between 2 and 8.

▶ Moving away from using concrete materials in order to combine these small quantities and towards the stage of using visualisation techniques to find the answers mentally.

Note to member of staff or parent

▶ Make sure the child is recognising the dice patterns, not counting the dice spots.

▶ Make sure the child is not adding by counting in ones, on fingers or otherwise.

▶ Be sure to talk about what is going on at each step, especially when either player puts two components together to make 5.

▶ At first, prepare two game boards to suit the size of your counters.

▶ After playing a few times, preferably on different occasions, try the more abstract version of the game using the two boards on the next page.

Equipment needed

Two 6-sided spot dice, altered as follows: cover the patterns of 5 and 6 with a sticker and cover the stickers on one die with one pattern of 2 and one pattern of 3, and on the other die with one pattern of 4 and one pattern of 1. Counters in two colours (later, coloured pencils in two colours). Two paper game boards on which are drawn five patterns of 5 making sure the drawn circles roughly match the size of your counters.

2. Collect 5s

Name:

Date:

When to hand it in:

Instructions

Preparation: Attach stickers to each of two 6-sided spot dice, so that the numbers 5 and 6 are covered and replaced by the numbers 2 and 3 on one die, and by 4 and 1 on the other.

Rules: Take turns to throw both dice together and announce the total. If the total is any number other than 5, that is the end of your turn. If the total is 5, take counters of one colour to match one die throw and counters of the other colour to match the other die. Use the counters to cover one complete pattern of 5 on your board as follows: for components 4 + 1 it is the central spot that must be in a different colour to those forming the outer square; for components 2 + 3, the three counters of the same colour should be arranged along one of the diagonals in the pattern of 5. The winner is the first player to cover all 5 of the patterns of 5.

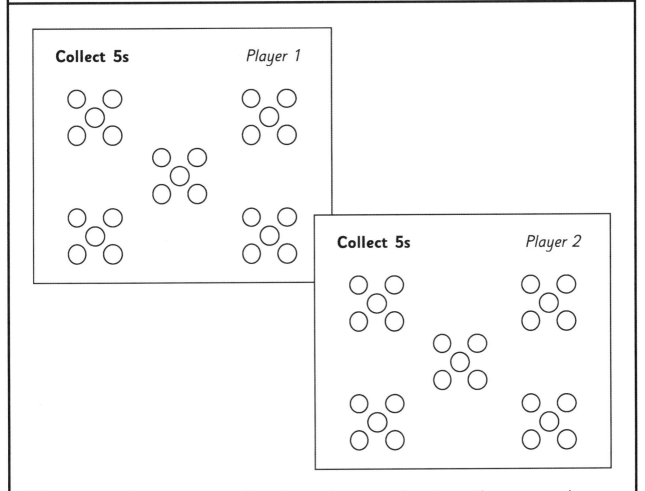

Play again without counters: After playing the game a few times with counters on larger boards, play it with two colours of pencils instead on the boards above. Use the same dice as before. Shade in the patterns of 5 every time your dice add up to 5, using different colours to represent each die throw just as you did when playing with the counters.

3   Clear the Deck of 6s – a game for 1 player

Teaching points

▶ Components of 6. There are only three ways of building the number 6 from two components.

▶ The connection between addition, subtraction and missing addend problems.

▶ Mental addition of two numbers up to a total of 10.

Note to member of staff or parent

▶ Make sure the child knows that adding in ones, on fingers or otherwise, is not allowed.

▶ As the child picks up pairs of cards during play, both numbers should be spoken aloud.

▶ Make sure the target number is spelled out clearly. Although the layout of the cards makes no difference to the game, an arrangement of two rows of three may act as a reminder of this game's target number, which is 6.

▶ The game should be played more than once and on more than one occasion. Encourage the child to keep playing until the components of 6 are easily recognised, rather than calculated.

Equipment needed

A pack of cards made up of four each of the numbers 1 to 5 inclusive. If you have no digit cards, remove the appropriate cards from a standard pack of playing cards and treat the Aces as 1s.

3. Clear the Deck of 6s

Name:

Date:

Instructions

Use a pack of cards made up of four each of the numbers 1 to 5 inclusive. Shuffle the cards and lay out five of them face up, arranged as shown below. Put the remaining cards together in a pack face down at the bottom right-hand corner of the array.

Clear away any two cards that add up to the target number of 6. As you pick up the cards, name both the numbers aloud. Fill the two empty spaces with new cards from the top of the pack and continue in the same way, searching for pairs of components of 6.

The game is won if you manage to clear all the cards in the pack.

Clear the Deck of 6s   **A Solitaire Game**

4   3-in-a-Line Dominoes – a game for 2 players

Teaching points

▶ The key components of all the numbers up to 10. The words 'key components' refer to the doubles and near-doubles facts, e.g. 4 and 4 are the key components of 8.

▶ The numbers 1 to 5 (but not 6) are key components of the numbers up to 10.

▶ The same small number can be one of the key components of up to three larger numbers, e.g. the number 4 is one of the key components of 7 and of 8 and of 9.

▶ The commutativity of addition, i.e. when combining two numbers it does not matter which is taken first.

Note to member of staff or parent

▶ Make sure the child is recognising the dice patterns, not counting the dice spots.

▶ The child should be able to identify the total value of each domino without having to count or add in ones. Encourage a lot of talk about component values and total values.

▶ Be sure to explain the rule that, whatever the throw of the dice, that pattern must be taken as a whole, e.g. a throw of 4 cannot be split into smaller components: a throw of 4 can only result in the player shading in one of the components of the number 7 or of the number 8 or of the number 9, and if all four of the 4s on the board are already shaded the player misses the turn.

▶ Make sure the number patterns created during the preparation stage are drawn as small circles, not dots, so that they can be coloured in during play. After preparing the game board, each column should look like a vertical arrangement of this:

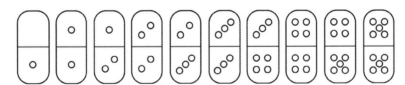

▶ As there is not much space inside the domino shapes on the next page, you may prefer to create larger game boards on paper. Simply sketch ten blank dominoes arranged in either a vertical or a horizontal line for each player.

Equipment needed

An ordinary 6-sided spot die. Paper and pencil.

4. 3-in-a-Line Dominoes

Name:

Date:

When to hand it in:

Instructions

Preparation: Draw small empty circles into the blank domino shapes below, to create the key component dot patterns for the numbers 1 to 10, in order (ascending or descending).

Rules: Take turns to throw a die and throw again if you get a 6. Match the throw of the die by shading in the empty circles of the same pattern in any one place that the pattern appears on one half of a domino. The winner is the first to shade in three whole consecutive dominoes, i.e. to complete all the components contributing to three consecutive numbers.

3-in-a-Line   *Player 1*

Dominoes

3-in-a-Line   *Player 2*

Dominoes

5 Dot Pattern Stickers Race – a game for 2 or 3 players

Teaching points

▶ Dot patterns for numbers up to 10 that are based on doubles and near-doubles facts, i.e. the key component facts.

▶ Matching digits to dot patterns.

▶ A stage in the transition from concrete materials to more abstract representations by using stickers rather than counters and digits rather than spot dice.

Please note that before playing this game, children should already be familiar with dot patterns for all the numbers up to 10, and should have had plenty of experience of using concrete materials to create and explore the patterns.

Note to member of staff or parent

▶ Make sure the child uses only the dot patterns that are shown here. It does not matter if the patterns are made horizontally or vertically or upside-down, nor if the three dots from the pattern of 7 are arranged in a straight line or as a diagonal.

▶ Ask the child to teach you the necessary dot patterns before the game starts (even if you already know them).

▶ When taking stickers from the sheet, the child should engage in the minimum amount of counting, e.g. if the die shows 8, the child can take all but two of the stickers in one row.

▶ When creating the dot patterns on the next page, remind the child to put the stickers close together within each pattern so as to leave room for all the numbers from one game.

▶ Players each need a separate piece of paper on which to stick their number patterns.

▶ Encourage lots of talk about how the numbers are built out of their two key components.

Equipment needed

100 or 150 (depending on the number of players) small round self-adhesive stickers, all in the same colour. A piece of paper for each opponent. A 6-sided die on which the digits – note digits, not dots – for the numbers 4 to 9 appear once each (use a blank die or an ordinary die covered with stickers on which to write the numbers).

5. Dot Pattern Stickers Race

Name:

Date:

When to hand it in:

Instructions

Preparation: Take self-adhesive small round stickers and allocate 5 lines of 10 dots to each player, using scissors to cut the backing sheet if necessary. Alter a die to show all the numbers from 4 to 9 inclusive, as digits (not dot patterns).

Rules: Players take turns to throw the die and take the number of stickers to match the throw. Arrange the stickers to create the doubles or near-doubles dot pattern for the number. Put the stickers close together within each pattern so that several numbers can fit on the page. At the end of the game it is not necessary to wait for an exact throw of the die. The winner is the first player to use up, or run out of, all 50 dot stickers.

Dot Pattern Stickers Race

Player 1

6 Components & Key Components [5–10] – a game for 2 or 3 players

Teaching points

▶ The components and the key components of the numbers 5 to 10.

▶ The commutativity of addition, i.e. 2 + 3 is equal in value to 3 + 2.

▶ Mental addition of two small numbers to create a total of 10 or less.

Note to member of staff or parent

▶ Make sure the child is recognising the dice patterns, not counting the dice spots.

▶ Make sure the child understands the term 'key components' to refer to number bonds that are also doubles and near-doubles facts, i.e. the key component facts of the numbers 5 to 10 are: 2 + 3, 3 + 3, 3 + 4, 4 + 4, 4 + 5 and 5 + 5.

▶ Ask the child to teach you the key components (even if you already know them).

▶ In preparation for the game, players choose 6 digits choosing between the numbers 5 to 10 inclusive, to create their own game board. The choice of digits is a free choice. So, a player might wish to write the same number in each box, or write a different number in each box, or write some repeated numbers and omit other numbers altogether. The numbers may be written in ascending order, descending order, or no order at all.

▶ During the game, discuss the fact that if either dice shows a 6 it must be thrown again because 6 is not a key component of any of the numbers up to 10.

▶ Encourage plenty of talk about how to combine the dice totals without counting. For example, if the dice show 2 and 4, the child can reason that the answer must be 6 from their knowledge of the key facts of 5 (i.e. 2 + 3) or of 7 (i.e. 3 + 4), or by visualising the dice pattern of 6 and seeing within it a pattern of 4 and a pattern of 2, or by knowing that adding 2 to any number will be not the next number in the counting sequence but the one after that.

▶ The game is suitable for more than 2 players.

▶ The game should be played more than once and on more than one occasion.

Equipment needed

Two ordinary 6-sided spot dice. Two coloured pencils in two different colours.

6. Components & Key Components [5–10]

Name:

Date:

When to hand it in:

Instructions

Preparation: Players write a number inside each of the six boxes on their own game board below, choosing freely between the numbers 5 to 10 inclusive. Decide which of the two colours of pencils will be used for the key component facts and use it to colour in the letters of the words key components here (to help remember which colour is which).

Rules: Players take turns to throw both dice. If you get a 6, throw the die again. Add the two dice numbers mentally and announce the total. If the total matches a digit in one of your boxes, shade that box using the relevant coloured pencil, depending on whether you had to add key components to reach the total, or not. If you have no matching box, or one that is already shaded, you can do nothing on this turn.

The winner is the first player with any three boxes shaded in the colour for key component facts, or the first with five out of the six boxes shaded in any colour, whichever happens first.

Components & Key Components [5–10]   *Player 1*

◻ ◻ ◻ ◻ ◻ ◻

Components & Key Components [5–10]   *Player 2*

◻ ◻ ◻ ◻ ◻ ◻

The Dyscalculia Resource Book © Ronit Bird, 2011 (SAGE)

7   Regroup – a game for 2 players

Teaching points

▶ Exploring the possible component pairs, or number bonds, of any number up to 10.

▶ The connection between addition, subtraction and missing addend problems.

▶ Practice in visualisation of small amounts.

▶ Using logic to derive a new fact that is one reasoning step away from a known fact, e.g. reasoning that 3 + 5 must be equal to the same total as 4 + 4.

Please note that children should have had previous concrete experience of creating numbers out of two groups of counters or nuggets in order to explore what happens when one unit is moved from one group to the other.

Note to member of staff or parent

▶ Make sure the child is recognising the dice patterns, not counting the dice spots.

▶ When adding amounts, the child is not allowed to count in ones, on fingers or otherwise. The whole point of this game is to develop logical reasoning in order to derive new addition or subtraction facts from known facts.

▶ Make sure the child understands the term 'triad' to refer to three numbers arranged so that the number at the top is equal in value to the sum of the two numbers below.

▶ Explain to the child that this is a guessing game and that incorrect guesses are simply bad luck.

▶ Provide a screen, such as a large book or box file, behind which both players can hide their dice throws and scrap paper during play.

▶ The game board provides space to record five turns each but, if both players' score is the same after five turns, play on until one player emerges as a clear winner.

▶ The game should be played more than once and on more than one occasion.

Equipment needed

Scrap paper and pencil. Tokens for scoring. Three 6-sided spot dice altered so that the single spot, i.e. the number 1, is covered by the dot pattern for 7 on one die, the pattern for 8 on another die and the pattern for 9 on the third die. The three substituted dot patterns should look like these:

7. Regroup

Name:

Date:

When to hand it in:

Instructions

Preparation: Alter the 1s on three 6-sided spot dice to a 7, an 8 and a 9.

Rules: Two players take turns to throw all three dice, hiding them from the other player. Discard the die showing the smallest amount and make a hidden note on scrap paper of the other two numbers. Mentally add the numbers on the two dice, and write the total at the top of one of the triad shapes on your game board. Next, visualise one spot moving from one die face to the other, and write the two newly visualised components at the bottom of the triad. E.g. if you throw two 4s (having discarded the third die), write 8 at the top and 3 + 5 (or 5 + 3) at the bottom, as shown here. The second player uses this written clue to guess the two original components. A correct guess (4 + 4 in this example) wins a token for the second player; an incorrect guess (6 + 2 in this example) wins a token for the first player. The winner has most tokens.

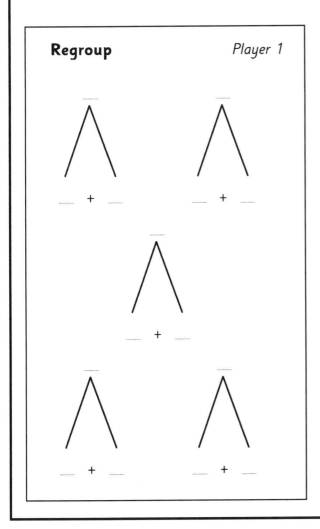

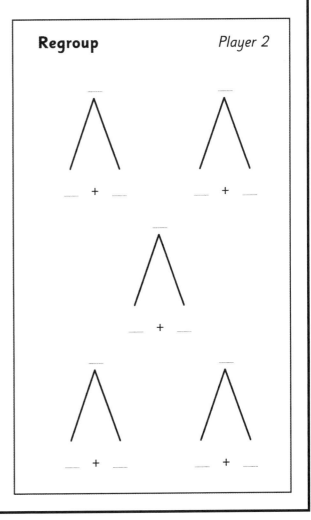

8   Twos & Threes – a game for 2 players

Teaching points

▶ Adding 2 and 3 to other small numbers.

▶ The commutativity of addition, i.e. 2 + 3 is equal in value to 3 + 2.

▶ The 'difference' between numbers can be expressed as addition as well as subtraction.

▶ The connection between subtraction and missing addend problems.

Note to member of staff or parent

▶ Make sure the child is using knowledge of components, or number bonds, and is not counting in ones.

▶ Allow the child to discover for him/herself that only a difference of 2 or 3 will translate into a sum of the type needed for this game.

▶ Encourage the child to read aloud each recorded number sentence, leaving it up to the child to judge whether the sum makes sense, i.e. it is the child's job (rather than yours) to check whether the right numbers have been copied into the right boxes.

▶ The game should be played more than once and on more than one occasion.

Equipment needed

A pack of cards made up of four each of the numbers 4 to 10 inclusive. If you have no digit cards, remove the appropriate cards from a standard pack of playing cards.

8. Twos & Threes

Name:

Date:

When to hand it in:

Instructions

Shuffle a pack of cards made up of four each of the numbers 4 to 10 inclusive. Players take turns to pick up two cards at a time from the pack and announce the difference between the numbers. Have another turn if the two cards you pick up are the same. If it is possible, complete one of the number sentences on your board by copying the two numbers from the cards into the empty boxes of one sum. Replace the cards in a new pile. The winner is the first player to complete all six sums on their board. Alternatively, once the pack has been gone through twice (shuffle the cards again before reusing), the winner is the player with the most number sentences completed.

Twos & Threes   *Player 1*

☐ + 2 = ☐   2 + ☐ = ☐   ☐ = 2 + ☐

☐ + 3 = ☐   3 + ☐ = ☐   ☐ = 3 + ☐

Twos & Threes   *Player 2*

☐ + 2 = ☐   2 + ☐ = ☐   ☐ = 2 + ☐

☐ + 3 = ☐   3 + ☐ = ☐   ☐ = 3 + ☐

The Dyscalculia Resource Book © Ronit Bird, 2011 (SAGE)

9 Component Su Doku Puzzle

Teaching points

▶ Combining small components to create numbers up to 9.

▶ Splitting numbers into chunks, i.e. into components, or number bonds.

▶ The connection between addition, subtraction and missing addend problems.

▶ Logical reasoning.

Note to member of staff or parent

▶ The child should begin by answering the questions in the Tips section. Make sure the child thinks about each question and is not simply copying the answers from a previous puzzle.

▶ The Tips section must be folded back so that the answers are hidden before the child starts to solve the puzzle.

▶ There must be no adding or subtracting by counting in ones, on fingers or otherwise.

▶ The child may choose any way of distinguishing between possible answers and final answers, but may like to know that a commonly used method is to write the possibilities very lightly and very small and to rub out these digits once a conclusion has been reached about any square.

▶ The child should use only logic. The puzzles in this book have been carefully designed so that the solver need never resort to guesswork or trial and error.

Equipment needed

A pencil and rubber.

9. Component Su Doku Puzzle

Name:

Date:

When to hand it in:

Instructions

Complete the Su Doku grid so that the numbers 1 to 5 appear once in each column and each row. The rectangular boxes enclose two different components that add up to the number at the top left of the box.

Tips: Work out these facts first:

· Each row and each column must add up to _____ (i.e. 1 + 2 + 3 + 4 + 5).

· There is only one way to build the number 3 :   3 = _____ + _____ .

· There is only one way to build the number 4 :   4 = _____ + _____ .   (Why can't you use 2 + 2?)

· There are only two possible ways to build the number 5, namely _____ + _____ or _____ + _____ .

· The largest possible number is _____ because it is created by adding _____ and _____ .

· The next largest possible number is _____ because it is created by adding _____ and _____ .

Component Su Doku Puzzle   Digits 1 to 5

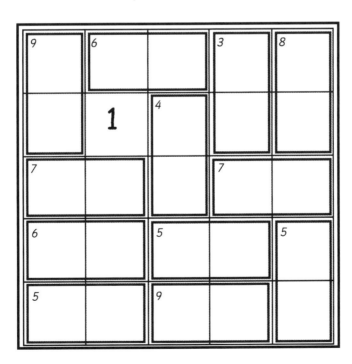

10 Spotlight on 7 and 8 – a game for 1 player

Teaching points

▶ Components of 7 and 8. There are only three different ways of building the number 7, and four different ways of building the number 8, from two components.

▶ The connection between addition, subtraction and missing addend problems.

▶ Mental addition of two numbers up to a total of 14.

Note to member of staff or parent

▶ Make sure the child knows that adding in ones, on fingers or otherwise, is not allowed.

▶ As the child picks up pairs of cards during play, both numbers should be spoken aloud together with the target number that they total.

▶ The game should be played more than once and on more than one occasion. Encourage the child to keep playing until the components of both 7 and 8 are easily recognised, rather than calculated.

▶ The child should be told that it is impossible to clear all the cards in this solitaire game. The minimum possible cards left at the end of a game is 2, so any score lower than 6 can be considered a good score.

Equipment needed

A pack of cards made up of four each of the numbers 1 to 7 inclusive. If you have no digit cards, remove the appropriate cards from a standard pack of playing cards and treat the Aces as 1s.

10. Spotlight on 7 and 8

Name:

Date:

Instructions

Use a pack of cards made up of four each of the numbers 1 to 7 inclusive. Shuffle the cards and lay out eight of them face up, as shown below. Put the remaining cards together in a pack face down in the middle of the array.

The aim is to clear away any two cards that add up to the target numbers of 7 or 8, while alternating the targets. Beginning with whichever number you please, the next pair of cards to be cleared must total the other target number. As you play, name both components and their total aloud before filling the gaps with two new cards from the pack at the centre.

Keep a record of how many cards remain at the end of each game and try to beat your own record next time. Any score of fewer than 6 cards remaining is a good score.

Spotlight on 7 and 8   **A Solitaire Game**

11   Component Su Doku Puzzle

Teaching points

▶ Combining small components to create numbers up to 9.

▶ Splitting numbers into chunks, i.e. into components, or number bonds.

▶ The connection between addition, subtraction and missing addend problems.

▶ Logical reasoning.

Note to member of staff or parent

▶ The child should begin by answering the questions in the Tips section. Make sure the child thinks about each question and is not simply copying the answers from a previous puzzle.

▶ The Tips section must be folded back so that the answers are hidden before the child starts to solve the puzzle.

▶ There must be no adding or subtracting by counting in ones, on fingers or otherwise.

▶ The child may choose any way of distinguishing between possible answers and final answers, but may like to know that a commonly used method is to write the possibilities very lightly and very small and to rub out these digits once a conclusion has been reached about any square.

▶ The child should use only logic. The puzzles in this book have been carefully designed so that the solver need never resort to guesswork or trial and error.

Equipment needed

A pencil and rubber.

11. Component Su Doku Puzzle

Name:

Date:

When to hand it in:

Instructions

Complete the Su Doku grid so that the numbers 1 to 5 appear once in each column and each row. The rectangular boxes enclose two different components that add up to the number at the top left of the box.

Tips: Work out these facts first:

· Each row and each column must add up to _____ (i.e. 1 + 2 + 3 + 4 + 5).

· There is only one way to build the number 3 :   3 =____ + ____ .

· There is only one way to build the number 4 :   4 =____ + ____ .

· There are only two possible ways to build the number 5, namely ____ + ____ or ____ + ____ .

· The largest possible number is ____ because it is created by adding ____ and ____ .

· The next largest possible number is ____ because it is created by adding ____ and ____ .

Component Su Doku Puzzle

Digits 1 to 5

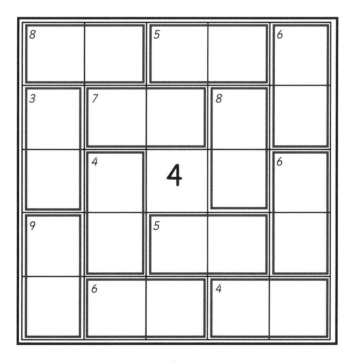

12   Odd or Even Domino Ladders – a game for 2 players

Teaching points

▶ Odd and even numbers between 1 and 10.

▶ Adding two odd numbers, or two even numbers, always creates an even number.

▶ Adding an odd to an even number always creates an odd number.

▶ Mental addition using component knowledge up to 6 + 6.

Note to member of staff or parent

▶ Make sure the child is using knowledge of components and is not counting in ones.

▶ Make sure the child knows which numbers are odd and which are even. If recognition is not secure, have the child use counters to build each of the dot patterns in turn from 2 to 10. Once a pattern is complete, the child should rearrange the counters into pairs and notice that the odd numbers always have one counter left over. So, if there is an '*odd* one out' that does not belong to a pair, the number must be an *odd number*.

▶ You may need to redraw the game boards in order for the dominoes you use to fit on top of the numbered spaces in the ladders.

▶ Play the game at least twice so that the child has a chance to focus on both odd and even numbers, in turn.

▶ Play a variation of the game, in which both players try to collect the full range of numbers between 1 and 10. In this version, each player announces the total of whichever domino they pick up, as well as the odd or even facts about the components and about the total. The winner is the player with four dominoes in a row on either one of their ladders.

Equipment needed

A set of dominoes. A normal European set has 28 stones ranging from 0-0 to 6-6.

12. Odd or Even Domino Ladders

Name:

Date:

Instructions

Player 1 uses the ladder showing odd numbers while Player 2 uses the ladder showing even numbers. Mix a set of dominoes thoroughly, face down. Players take turns to pick up a domino and must say whether each of the patterns on either side is odd or even and whether the total is odd or even. If the total is odd, it is up to Player 1 to announce the actual total value of the domino (no matter whose turn it is) and if the total is even, Player 2 must announce the total. The player whose turn it is may now place the domino on their own ladder if the total matches one of the numbers shown between the rungs. If not, the domino is discarded. The winner is the first player with four dominoes in a row.

Variation: Draw two ladders for each player so that both have an odd and an even ladder.

Odd or Even Domino Ladders

ODD numbers   *Player 1*

| 9 |
| 7 |
| 5 |
| 3 |
| 1 |

Odd or Even Domino Ladders

EVEN numbers   *Player 2*

| 10 |
| 8 |
| 6 |
| 4 |
| 2 |

13   Component Su Doku Puzzle

Teaching points

▶ Combining small components to create numbers up to 9.

▶ Splitting numbers into chunks, i.e. into components, or number bonds.

▶ The connection between addition, subtraction and missing addend problems.

▶ Logical reasoning.

Note to member of staff or parent

▶ The child should begin by answering the questions in the Tips section. Make sure the child thinks about each question and is not simply copying the answers from a previous puzzle.

▶ The Tips section must be folded back so that the answers are hidden before the child starts to solve the puzzle.

▶ There must be no adding or subtracting by counting in ones, on fingers or otherwise.

▶ The child may choose any way of distinguishing between possible answers and final answers, but may like to know that a commonly used method is to write the possibilities very lightly and very small and to rub out these digits once a conclusion has been reached about any square.

▶ The child should use only logic. The puzzles in this book have been carefully designed so that the solver need never resort to guesswork or trial and error.

Equipment needed

A pencil and rubber.

13. Component Su Doku Puzzle

Name:

Date:

When to hand it in:

Instructions

Complete the Su Doku grid so that the numbers 1 to 5 appear in each column and each row. The rectangular boxes enclose two different components that add up to the number at the top left of the box.

Tips: Work out these facts first:

· Each row and each column must add up to _____ .

· The smallest possible number is _____ and must be made of _____ and _____ .

· The next smallest possible number is _____ and must be made of _____ and _____ .

· The largest possible number is _____ and must be made of _____ and _____ .

· The next largest possible number is _____ and must be made of _____ and _____ .

Component Su Doku Puzzle

Digits 1 to 5

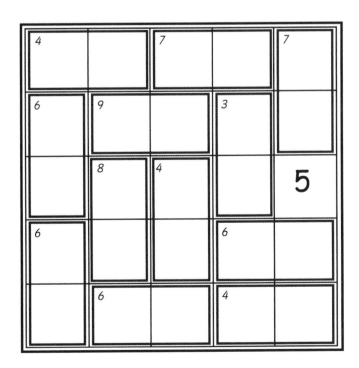

14   Odds & Evens Circuit – a game for 2 players

Teaching points

▶ Odd and even numbers between 1 and 10.

▶ Clockwise and anticlockwise.

Note to member of staff or parent

▶ Make sure the child knows which numbers are odd and which are even. If recognition is not secure, have the child use counters to build each of the dot patterns in turn from 2 to 10. Once a pattern is complete, the child should rearrange the counters into pairs and notice that the odd numbers always have one counter left over. So, if there is an '*odd* one out' that does not belong to a pair, the number must be an *odd number*.

▶ Put a clock or watch with a second hand in full view, so that the child can consult it if unsure about the direction of a clockwise or anticlockwise move.

▶ The game should be played more than once and on more than one occasion.

▶ The variation, using the numbers 5 to 10 (alter the numbers on the die by attaching stickers to its faces), is a more challenging version of the game.

Equipment needed

An ordinary 6-sided die. Two tokens.

14. Odds & Evens Circuit

Name:

Date:

Instructions

Two players each move a token along the same game board, below, starting at the shaded hexagon in the centre. Take turns to throw a die. If the number is even, move the token in a clockwise direction the number of spaces that matches the throw, e.g. if the first die throw is 2, move the token two spaces up and to the right of the centre. If the number is odd, move the token in an anticlockwise direction the number of spaces that matches the throw. At any time that your token passes through (rather than lands on) the central shaded hexagon, you may choose to continue in either of the two available paths that lie ahead. The winner is the first player whose token lands on the central shaded hexagon.

Variation: Alter the die to show the numbers 5 to 10 inclusive.

Odds & Evens Circuit

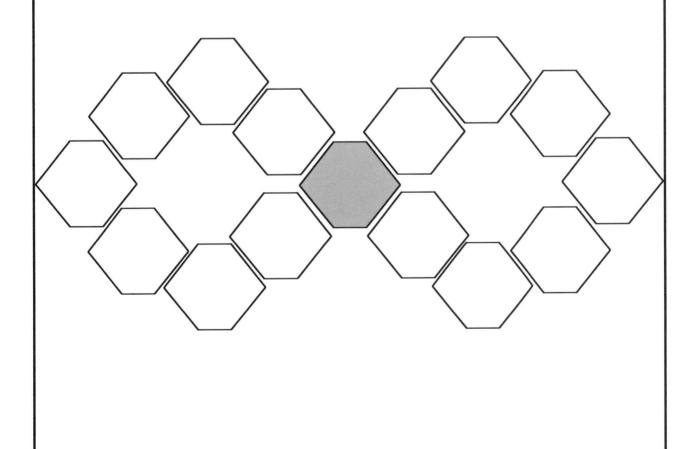

15 Component Su Doku Puzzle

Teaching points

▶ Combining small components to create numbers up to 9.

▶ Splitting numbers into chunks, i.e. into components, or number bonds.

▶ The connection between addition, subtraction and missing addend problems.

▶ Logical reasoning.

Note to member of staff or parent

▶ The child should begin by answering the questions in the Tips section. Make sure the child thinks about each question and is not simply copying the answers from a previous puzzle.

▶ The Tips section must be folded back so that the answers are hidden before the child starts to solve the puzzle.

▶ There must be no adding or subtracting by counting in ones, on fingers or otherwise.

▶ The child may choose any way of distinguishing between possible answers and final answers, but may like to know that a commonly used method is to write the possibilities very lightly and very small and to rub out these digits once a conclusion has been reached about any square.

▶ The child should use only logic. The puzzles in this book have been carefully designed so that the solver need never resort to guesswork or trial and error.

Equipment needed

A pencil and rubber.

15. Component Su Doku Puzzle

Name:

Date:

When to hand it in:

Instructions
Complete the Su Doku grid so that the numbers 1 to 5 appear in each column and each row. The rectangular boxes enclose two different components that add up to the number at the top left of the box.

Tips: Work out these facts first:

· Each row and each column must add up to _____ .

· The smallest possible number is _____ and must be made of _____ and _____ .

· The next smallest possible number is _____ and must be made of _____ and _____ .

· The largest possible number is _____ and must be made of _____ and _____ .

· The next largest possible number is _____ and must be made of _____ and _____ .

Component Su Doku Puzzle

Digits 1 to 5

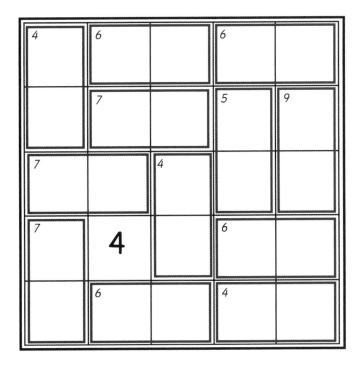

16 Clear the Deck of 9s – a game for 1 player

Teaching points

◗ Components of 9. There are only four ways of building the number 9 from two components.

◗ The connection between addition, subtraction and missing addend problems.

◗ Mental addition of two numbers up to a total of 16.

Note to member of staff or parent

◗ Make sure the child knows that adding in ones, on fingers or otherwise, is not allowed.

◗ As the child picks up pairs of cards during play, both numbers should be spoken aloud.

◗ Make sure the target number is spelled out clearly. Although the layout of the cards makes no difference to the game, an arrangement of three rows of three may act as a reminder that the target number is 9.

◗ The game should be played more than once and on more than one occasion. Encourage the child to keep playing until the components of 9 are recognised, rather than calculated.

◗ The solitaire game Clear The Deck, which is presented here with a target of 9 and has been presented previously with a target of 6, can be adapted to practise the components of any of the numbers between 6 and 11. Please note that the components of 10 – otherwise known as complements to 10 – are particularly important to know well. In order to adapt the game to the target number of your choice, play with digit cards up to, but not including, the target number and lay out however many cards matches the highest number contained in the pack. Make sure the target number is spelled out clearly during each game.

Equipment needed

A pack of cards made up of four each of the numbers 1 to 8 inclusive. If you have no digit cards, remove the appropriate cards from a standard pack of playing cards and treat the Aces as 1s.

16. Clear the Deck of 9s

Name:

Date:

Instructions

Use a pack of cards made up of four each of the numbers 1 to 8 inclusive. Shuffle the cards and lay out eight of them face up, arranged as shown below. Put the remaining cards together in a pack face down at the bottom right-hand corner of the array.

Clear away any two cards that add up to the target number of 9. As you pick up the cards, name both the numbers aloud. Fill the two empty spaces with new cards from the top of the pack and continue in the same way, searching for pairs of components of 9.

The game is won if you manage to clear all the cards in the pack.

Clear the Deck of 9s   **A Solitaire Game**

17   Component Su Doku Puzzle

Teaching points

▶ Combining small components to create numbers up to 11.

▶ Splitting numbers into chunks, i.e. into components, or number bonds.

▶ The connection between addition, subtraction and missing addend problems.

▶ Logical reasoning.

Note to member of staff or parent

▶ The child should begin by answering the questions in the Tips section. Make sure the child thinks about each question and is not simply copying the answers from a previous puzzle.

▶ The Tips section must be folded back so that the answers are hidden before the child starts to solve the puzzle.

▶ There must be no adding or subtracting by counting in ones, on fingers or otherwise.

▶ The child may choose any way of distinguishing between possible answers and final answers, but may like to know that a commonly used method is to write the possibilities very lightly and very small and to rub out these digits once a conclusion has been reached about any square.

▶ The child should use only logic. The puzzles in this book have been carefully designed so that the solver need never resort to guesswork or trial and error.

Equipment needed

A pencil and rubber.

17. Component Su Doku Puzzle

Name:

Date:

When to hand it in:

Instructions

Complete the Su Doku grid so that the numbers 2 to 6 appear in each column and each row. The rectangular boxes enclose two different components that add up to the number at the top left of the box.

Tips: Work out these facts first:

· Each row and each column must add up to _____ .

· The smallest possible number is _____ and must be made of _____ and _____ .

· The next smallest possible number is _____ and must be made of _____ and _____ .

· The largest possible number is _____ and must be made of _____ and _____ .

· The next largest possible number is _____ and must be made of _____ and _____ .

Component Su Doku Puzzle

Digits 2 to 6

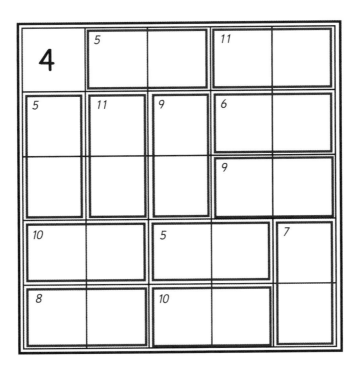

18   Equation Solitaire – a game for 1 player

Teaching points

▶ Find the difference between the two numbers by first sketching the problem as Cuisenaire rods and then recording the number relationships in writing.

Please note that children should not be asked to play this game unless they have had previous experience of working with the rods, including playing a concrete version of the game.

▶ Using diagrams as a bridge between concrete and abstract calculation.

▶ Formal recording of simple addition and subtraction equations.

▶ Components of numbers up to 10.

▶ The connection between addition, subtraction and missing number questions.

Note to member of staff or parent

▶ Make sure the child is familiar with Cuisenaire rods and can tell you all the colours and sizes in order: white, red, light green, purple, yellow, dark green, black, brown, blue, orange.

▶ Make sure the child understands the term 'equation' to mean any number sentence in which there is an equals sign. Remind the child that the number sentence is just as valid if the total comes first, e.g. $8 = 2 + 6$.

▶ The child does not need to draw the diagrammatic sketches exactly to scale, but should attempt a rough estimation of the lengths of the rods in relation to each other.

▶ The smaller rod can be sketched above or below the longer rod and it does not matter if the two rods are aligned at the left or at the right.

▶ The child should read the addition and subtraction facts aloud from the diagram, in any order or formulation desired, before attempting the harder task of recording the facts in writing on the game board.

Equipment needed

9 coloured pencils or pens to match the colours listed above. Please note that only 9 colours are needed because the smallest rod, white, is represented by an uncoloured square. In order to make recognition easier for the child, the purple should be a pinkish rather than a bluish purple, and the blue should be a dark blue.

18. Equation Solitaire

Name:

Date:

When to hand it in:

Instructions

Preparation: Colour the rods staircase below in the Cuisenaire colours. Do not label any rod with digits but remind yourself which colour is associated with each number.

Rules: Arrange the coloured pencils in two groups: one for the numbers 6 to 10, leaving the other four pencils in a second group. Pick one pencil from each group at random, with your eyes shut. Use the colours to sketch the relevant rods, one above the other and aligned at one end. Work out which rod you would need to place next to the smaller rod in order to equalise the length of the larger rod. Read aloud what you see in your sketch as one addition and one subtraction number sentence. Complete the two equations under your sketch. Watch out for the signs! The game is won if all your equations are correct and if every sketch is different (i.e. if you happen not to pick the same pair of colours twice).

$$8 = 6 + 2$$
$$8 - 2 = 6$$

Equation Solitaire

$$\square - \square = \square \qquad \square + \square = \square$$

$$\square = \square + \square \qquad \square - \square = \square$$

$$\square + \square = \square \qquad \square - \square = \square$$

$$\square = \square + \square \qquad \square = \square - \square$$

$$\square - \square = \square \qquad \square = \square + \square$$

$$\square - \square = \square \qquad \square + \square = \square$$

19   Component Su Doku Puzzle

Teaching points

▶ Combining small components to create numbers up to 11.

▶ Splitting numbers into chunks, i.e. into components, or number bonds.

▶ The connection between addition, subtraction and missing addend problems.

▶ Logical reasoning.

Note to member of staff or parent

▶ The child should begin by answering the questions in the Tips section. Make sure the child thinks about each question and is not simply copying the answers from a previous puzzle.

▶ The Tips section must be folded back so that the answers are hidden before the child starts to solve the puzzle.

▶ There must be no adding or subtracting by counting in ones, on fingers or otherwise.

▶ The child may choose any way of distinguishing between possible answers and final answers, but may like to know that a commonly used method is to write the possibilities very lightly and very small and to rub out these digits once a conclusion has been reached about any square.

▶ The child should use only logic. The puzzles in this book have been carefully designed so that the solver need never resort to guesswork or trial and error.

Equipment needed

A pencil and rubber.

19. Component Su Doku Puzzle

Name:

Date:

When to hand it in:

Instructions

Complete the Su Doku grid so that the numbers 2 to 6 appear in each column and each row. The rectangular boxes enclose two different components that add up to the number at the top left of the box.

Tips: Work out these facts first:

· Each row and each column must add up to _____ .

· The smallest possible number is _____ and must be made of _____ and _____ .

· The next smallest possible number is _____ and must be made of _____ and _____ .

· The largest possible number is _____ and must be made of _____ and _____ .

· The next largest possible number is _____ and must be made of _____ and _____ .

Component Su Doku Puzzle

Digits 2 to 6

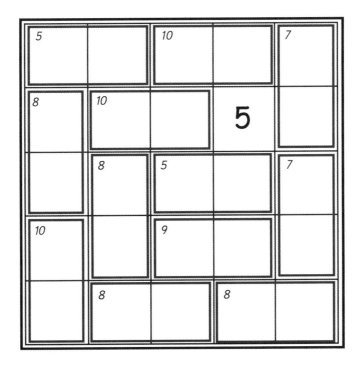

20 Cuisenaire Rods Wall Game – a game for 2 players

Teaching points

▶ Complements to 10.

▶ Using diagrams of Cuisenaire rods as a transition between concrete and more abstract work.

Please note that children should not be asked to play this game unless they have had previous experience of working with the rods, including playing a concrete version of the game.

Note to member of staff or parent

▶ Make sure the child is familiar with Cuisenaire rods and can tell you all the colours and sizes in order: white, red, light green, purple, yellow, dark green, black, brown, blue, orange.

▶ Make sure that the child understands the term 'complement' to mean the number that completes another to make 10.

▶ Make sure the child understands that $2 + 8 = 10$ and $8 + 2 = 10$ are two ways of expressing the same complement fact.

▶ Ask the child to tell you the 5 different complement facts (i.e. $9 + 1$, $8 + 2$, $7 + 3$, $6 + 4$ and $5 + 5$) in any order, and point out that all 5 of these facts have to be collected to win this game.

▶ The colouring of the rods on the game boards should be done lightly so that what is written on top will still be legible.

Equipment needed

9 coloured pencils or pens to match the colours listed above. Please note that only 9 colours are needed because the smallest rod, white, is represented by an uncoloured square. In order to make recognition easier for the child, the purple should be a pinkish rather than a bluish purple, and the blue should be a dark blue.

20. Cuisenaire Rods Wall Game

Name:

Date:

When to hand it in:

Instructions

Preparation: Each game board is a diagram of a Cuisenaire rods wall made of two staircases arranged side by side so as to highlight the 5 different pairs of numbers that add up to 10. Colour the rods, lightly, in the correct Cuisenaire colours on each player's wall.

Rules: Take turns to pick one of the 9 coloured pencils at random, with your eyes shut. Write the relevant complement fact on the colour that matches the pencil, before replacing the pencil. So, if you pick the red pencil, write 2 + 8 = 10 (or 8 + 2 = 10) on one area shaded red on your wall. If you pick a pencil for which you have already recorded both complement facts, or if you pick the orange pencil, you can do nothing on this turn. The winner is the first player to record all 5 different complement facts, i.e. 5 different pairs of numbers that total 10.

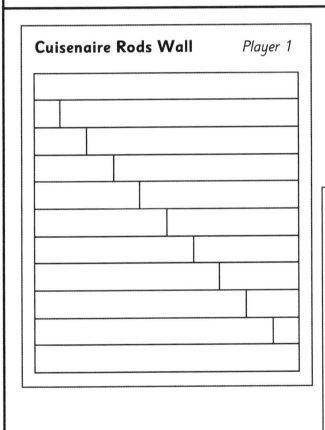

Cuisenaire Rods Wall *Player 1*

Cuisenaire Rods Wall *Player 2*

21 Component Su Doku Puzzle

Teaching points

▶ Combining small components to create numbers up to 11.

▶ Splitting numbers into chunks, i.e. into components, or number bonds.

▶ The connection between addition, subtraction and missing addend problems.

▶ Logical reasoning.

Note to member of staff or parent

▶ The child should begin by answering the questions in the Tips section. Make sure the child thinks about each question and is not simply copying the answers from a previous puzzle.

▶ The Tips section must be folded back so that the answers are hidden before the child starts to solve the puzzle.

▶ There must be no adding or subtracting by counting in ones, on fingers or otherwise.

▶ The child may choose any way of distinguishing between possible answers and final answers, but may like to know that a commonly used method is to write the possibilities very lightly and very small and to rub out these digits once a conclusion has been reached about any square.

▶ The child should use only logic. The puzzles in this book have been carefully designed so that the solver need never resort to guesswork or trial and error.

Equipment needed

A pencil and rubber.

21. Component Su Doku Puzzle

Name:

Date:

When to hand it in:

Instructions

Complete the Su Doku grid so that the numbers 2 to 6 appear in each column and each row. The rectangular boxes enclose two different components that add up to the number at the top left of the box.

Tips: Work out these facts first:

· Each row and each column must add up to _____ .

· The smallest possible number is _____ and must be made of _____ and _____ .

· The next smallest possible number is _____ and must be made of _____ and _____ .

· The largest possible number is _____ and must be made of _____ and _____ .

· The next largest possible number is _____ and must be made of _____ and _____ .

Component Su Doku Puzzle

Digits 2 to 6

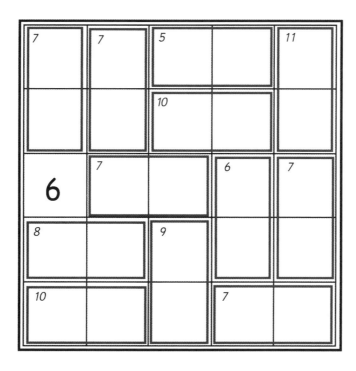

22 Triad Families – a game for 2 or 3 players

Teaching points

▶ Mental addition and subtraction of numbers up to 10.

▶ The connection between addition and subtraction.

▶ Informal versus formal methods of recording a number relationship.

Note to member of staff or parent

▶ Make sure there is no counting in ones, on fingers or otherwise.

▶ Make sure the term 'triad' is understood to mean an arrangement of three numbers such that the number at the top is equal in value to the sum of the two numbers below.

▶ The game should be played more than once and on more than one occasion.

▶ During one game, have the child use the blank space on the next page to record the game using the informal triad notation before using the more accepted notation for equations, as set out in the instructions on the next page. One equation should be expressed as addition and one as subtraction, but the order of the numbers is not important, i.e. for the example shown on the next page the child could choose to write $3 + 6 = 9$ or $6 + 3 = 9$ or $9 = 3 + 6$ or $9 = 6 + 3$ to record the relationship between the numbers expressed as addition, and either $9 - 3 = 6$ or $9 - 6 = 3$ to record the relationship between the numbers expressed as subtraction.

Equipment needed

A pack of cards made up of four each of the numbers 1 to 10 inclusive. If you have no digit cards, remove the appropriate cards from a standard pack of playing cards and treat the Aces as 1s.

22. Triad Families

Name:

Date:

When to hand it in:

Instructions

For each of the rounds in this game, shuffle a pack of digit cards and deal 12 cards face up to each player. Arrange as many of your cards as possible in triad family groups, so that the two numbers at the bottom of the triangular arrangement add up to the number at the top, e.g. the three cards 9, 6 and 3 can be arranged into a triad family group of cards as in the example shown here. Each correct triad scores one point. Play three more rounds. The winner is the first player to score 12 points, or the player with the highest score after four rounds of the game.

During the playing of any one game, record the families of facts from all four rounds, first informally using the triad notation, then formally as addition and subtraction equations.

$$9$$

$$3 \quad 6$$

$$9$$

$$3 + 6$$

$3 + 6 = 9$

$9 - 6 = 3$

Record one game of Triad Families

23   Component Su Doku Puzzle

Teaching points

▶ Combining small components to create numbers up to 11.

▶ Splitting numbers into chunks, i.e. into components, or number bonds.

▶ The connection between addition, subtraction and missing addend problems.

▶ Logical reasoning.

Note to member of staff or parent

▶ The child should begin by answering the questions in the Tips section. Make sure the child thinks about each question and is not simply copying the answers from a previous puzzle.

▶ The Tips section must be folded back so that the answers are hidden before the child starts to solve the puzzle.

▶ There must be no adding or subtracting by counting in ones, on fingers or otherwise.

▶ The child may choose any way of distinguishing between possible answers and final answers, but may like to know that a commonly used method is to write the possibilities very lightly and very small and to rub out these digits once a conclusion has been reached about any square.

▶ The child should use only logic. The puzzles in this book have been carefully designed so that the solver need never resort to guesswork or trial and error.

Equipment needed

A pencil and rubber.

23. Component Su Doku Puzzle

Name:

Date:

When to hand it in:

Instructions

Complete the Su Doku grid so that the numbers 2 to 6 appear in each column and each row. The rectangular boxes enclose two different components that add up to the number at the top left of the box.

Tips: Work out these facts first:

• Each row and each column must add up to _____ .

• The smallest possible number is _____ and must be made of _____ and _____ .

• The next smallest possible number is _____ and must be made of _____ and _____ .

• The largest possible number is _____ and must be made of _____ and _____ .

• The next largest possible number is _____ and must be made of _____ and _____ .

Component Su Doku Puzzle

Digits 2 to 6

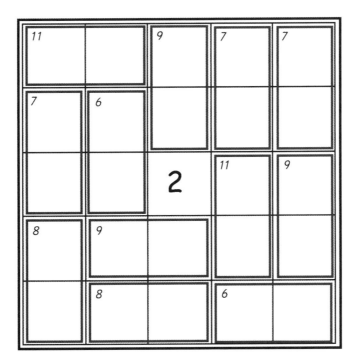

24   Banking Tens – a game for 2 or 3 players

Teaching points

▶ The complements of 10.

▶ Step counting in 10s.

▶ The informal triad method of recording an addition/subtraction number relationship.

▶ Informal versus formal methods of recording a simple equation.

▶ Having to think carefully about what the +, – and = signs mean.

Note to member of staff or parent

▶ Make sure there is no counting in ones, on fingers or otherwise.

▶ Make sure the term 'complement' is understood to mean the number that completes another to make 10.

▶ As the players put pairs of card in the bank, the numbers on the cards should be repeated aloud.

▶ The game should be played more than once and on more than one occasion.

▶ During one game, have the child use the blank space on the next page to record the game using the informal triad notation before recording the same information formally. One written equation should be expressed as addition and another as subtraction, and both equations should begin with the number 10 (this is to get the child to think carefully about the meaning of each of the signs). The order of the numbers beyond the equal sign is not important, i.e. for the example shown the child can choose to write 10 = 4 + 6 or 10 = 6 + 4, and 10 – 4 = 6 or 10 – 6 = 4.

Equipment needed

A pack of cards made up of four each of the numbers 1 to 9 inclusive. If you have no digit cards, remove the appropriate cards from a standard pack of playing cards and treat the Aces as 1s.

24. Banking Tens

Name:

Date:

When to hand it in:

Instructions

Preparation: Players write their names on a small piece of paper or card to represent their bank. Shuffle a pack consisting of 4 cards each of the numbers 1 to 9 and discard one at random without looking at it if there are only two players.

Rules: Deal 4 cards face up to each player. Take turns to pick up a new card from the pack and put it with your other cards. On your turn, look for complements, i.e. try to find any two numbers that make a total of 10. If you have a pair of complements, put both cards in the bank, by making a face-down pile on top of your name, and go straight on to have another turn. If you do not have a pair of complements, play passes to the next player. When all the cards have been used, players calculate their own score by adding the total value of the cards in their banked pile. This is much easier if you keep the cards in pairs during play because you know that each pair is worth 10. The winner is the player who has the most in the bank.

Below, record the pairs of cards you banked in any one game, first informally using the triad notation and then formally as addition and subtraction equations. Start each written equation with the number 10, as shown in the example here.

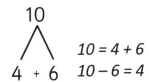

$$10 = 4 + 6$$
$$10 - 6 = 4$$

Record one game of Banking Tens

25 Bridging Race – a game for 2 or 3 players

Teaching points

▶ Bridging through 10.

▶ Combining knowledge of complements to 10 with knowledge of components up to 10.

▶ Recording on an empty number line.

Please note that this game has been designed for pupils who have already been taught about the bridging technique through concrete materials and who are now ready to move towards a more abstract way of working.

Note to member of staff or parent

▶ There must be no adding or subtracting by counting in ones, on fingers or otherwise.

▶ A knowledge of complements to 10 is needed for labelling the first bridging jump.

▶ A knowledge of components and partitioning is needed to complete the technique.

▶ On the game board on the next page, the jumps on the first number line have been lightly sketched as if they are of equal size, but players may prefer to alter the size of the jumps they draw so that they approximately reflect the relative sizes of the numbers.

▶ There is no need to record the position of zero on any number line, unless the child particularly wishes to. Do not model the recording of zero on your own game board.

▶ There is no need to put arrows on any jump, nor to add plus or minus signs to the numbers above the arcs that label the size of each jump.

▶ At the end of the game, encourage the child to look back over the recorded calculations on their own and one other player's board and to 'read' them aloud. This entails reading off the first number of the sum from the start of the number line and finding the second addend by mentally recombining the two jumps. The child will be able to supply the answer to the sum by reading it from the number line. Alternatively, hide the final number labels during the reading exercise and challenge the child to supply the answers anyway.

▶ The game should be played more than once and on more than one occasion.

Equipment needed

Two 6-sided digit dice, altered as follows (use sticky labels to cover the faces of an ordinary die or write on a blank die): replace the 1s and the 2s with a 7 and an 8 on one die and a 7 and a 9 on the other die. A paper game board and pencil for each player.

25. Bridging Race

Name:

Date:

When to hand it in:

Instructions

Preparation: Use two 6-sided digit dice, replacing the 1s and 2s with a 7 and an 8 on one die and a 7 and a 9 on the other. Draw game boards like the one below for each opponent.

Rules: Players take turns to throw both dice and announce whether the total is more or less than 10. If it is 10 or less, you can do nothing on this turn. If the total is more than 10, sketch the addition on a number line, labelling both jumps above the line and labelling the number line itself underneath the point at which a jump touches the line. If you throw the same pair of numbers again, you may swap the order of the numbers so as to make sure that no two of your number lines are identical (if you throw the same pair yet again, miss the turn). The winner is the first player to record five different bridging calculations on all five number lines.

Bridging Race   *Player 1*

26   Component Su Doku Puzzle

Teaching points

▶ Combining small components to create numbers up to 13.

▶ Splitting numbers into chunks, i.e. into components, or number bonds.

▶ The connection between addition, subtraction and missing addend problems.

▶ Logical reasoning.

Note to member of staff or parent

▶ The child should begin by answering the questions in the Tips section. Make sure the child thinks about each question and is not simply copying the answers from a previous puzzle.

▶ The Tips section must be folded back so that the answers are hidden before the child starts to solve the puzzle.

▶ There must be no adding or subtracting by counting in ones, on fingers or otherwise.

▶ The child should use only logic. The puzzles in this book have been carefully designed so that the solver need never resort to guesswork or trial and error.

Equipment needed

A pencil and rubber.

26. Component Su Doku Puzzle

Name:

Date:

When to hand it in:

Instructions
Complete the Su Doku grid so that the numbers 3 to 7 appear in each column and each row. The rectangular boxes enclose two different components that add up to the number at the top left of the box.

Tips: Work out these facts first:

• Each row and each column must add up to _____ .

• The smallest possible number is _____ and must be made of _____ and _____ .

• The next smallest possible number is _____ and must be made of _____ and _____ .

• The largest possible number is _____ and must be made of _____ and _____ .

• The next largest possible number is _____ and must be made of _____ and _____ .

Component Su Doku Puzzle

Digits 3 to 7

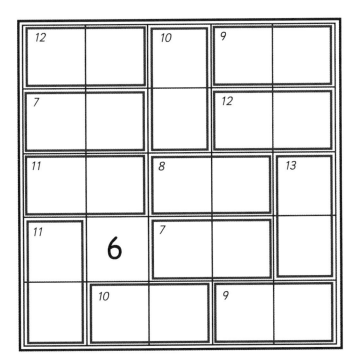

27   Addition Card War – a game for 2 players

Teaching points

▶ Mental addition of two numbers up to 12 or up to 20 when alternative card packs are used.

Note to member of staff or parent

▶ Make sure the child is using component knowledge or reasoning strategies to find the totals. Adding up in ones, on fingers or otherwise, is not allowed.

▶ The game should be played more than once and on more than one occasion.

▶ For variety, players can agree at the start of a game that the lower total will win all four cards in a round.

▶ During one game, have the child use the blank space on the next page to record the game. The recording can be in any form the child chooses, provided it shows all the rounds of one game and includes the totals of the pairs as well as the value of the individual cards that were played.

▶ Once this game becomes too easy, change the pack of cards for one made of eight each of the numbers 2 to 7 inclusive.

▶ When the child is ready, play Addition Card War with various different packs of cards. Three recommendations are:

(a) eight each of the numbers 3 to 8 inclusive,
(b) eight each of the numbers 4 to 9 inclusive, and
(c) six each of the numbers 3 to 10 inclusive.

Equipment needed

A pack of cards made up of eight each of the numbers 1 to 6 inclusive (or see above for various alternatives). If you have no digit cards, remove the appropriate cards from two standard packs of playing cards and treat the Aces as 1s.

27. Addition Card War

Name:

Date:

When to hand it in:

Instructions

Use a shuffled pack of cards made up of eight each of the numbers 1 to 6 inclusive. Split the pack between two players. On each turn, both players pick up two cards from the top of their pack and announce the total value of the pair. Whoever has the higher total wins all four cards. If the totals are equal, the four cards for that round remain on the table and are taken by the winner of the next round. The winner has most cards at the end of the game.

Variation: Play with a pack of cards containing eight each of the numbers 2 to 7 inclusive.

Record one game of Addition Card War

28 Component Su Doku Puzzle

Teaching points

▶ Combining small components to create numbers up to 13.

▶ Splitting numbers into chunks, i.e. into components, or number bonds.

▶ The connection between addition, subtraction and missing addend problems.

▶ Logical reasoning.

Note to member of staff or parent

▶ The child should begin by answering the questions in the Tips section. Make sure the child thinks about each question and is not simply copying the answers from a previous puzzle.

▶ The Tips section must be folded back so that the answers are hidden before the child starts to solve the puzzle.

▶ There must be no adding or subtracting by counting in ones, on fingers or otherwise.

▶ The child should use only logic. The puzzles in this book have been carefully designed so that the solver need never resort to guesswork or trial and error.

Equipment needed

A pencil and rubber.

28. Component Su Doku Puzzle

Name:

Date:

When to hand it in:

Instructions

Complete the Su Doku grid so that the numbers 3 to 7 appear in each column and each row. The rectangular boxes enclose two different components that add up to the number at the top left of the box.

Tips: Work out these facts first:

· Each row and each column must add up to _____ .

· The smallest possible number is _____ and must be made of _____ and _____ .

· The next smallest possible number is _____ and must be made of _____ and _____ .

· The largest possible number is _____ and must be made of _____ and _____ .

· The next largest possible number is _____ and must be made of _____ and _____ .

Component Su Doku Puzzle

Digits 3 to 7

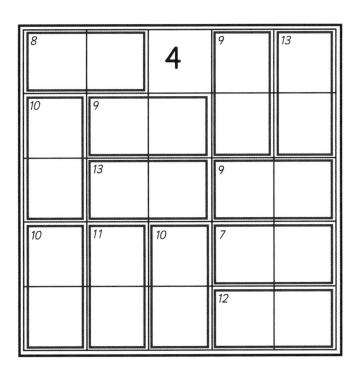

29   Domino Bonus Game – a game for 2 players

Teaching points

▸ Recognising and matching dot patterns.

▸ Mental addition of pairs of numbers up to 12.

▸ The equal sign means 'is equal in value to'. It does not mean 'now find the answer'.

▸ Formal notation of an equation that has addition signs on both sides.

Note to member of staff or parent

▸ Make sure that the child uses knowledge of components throughout and makes no attempt to add in ones, on fingers or otherwise.

▸ Encourage repeated mention of the total value, as well as the component parts, of the various domino stones in play.

▸ The game should be played more than once and on more than one occasion.

▸ During one game, have the child use the blank space on the next page to record diagrammatically the pairs of dominoes that feature in both players' bonus moves. At the end of the game, the child should record the same facts as a formal equation underneath the diagram. For example, the recording of one pair might look like this:

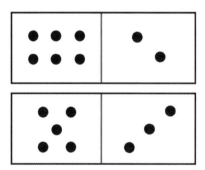

$$6 + 2 = 5 + 3$$

Equipment needed

A set of dominoes. A normal European set has 28 stones ranging from 0-0 to 6-6.

29. Domino Bonus Game

Name:

Date:

When to hand it in:

Instructions

Mix the 28 stones of a set of dominoes face down. Take 8 dominoes each, keeping them hidden. Whoever has the 6-6 starts or, failing that, the person with the next highest double. The second player places a domino at one end of the stone on the table so that the dot patterns match where the adjacent stones touch, just as in any normal game of dominoes.

What is different about this game is that each player has the chance to make a second, extra bonus move on each turn. As a bonus move, you may play a second stone from your hand by placing it at right angles to any domino with the same total number of spots. E.g. you may place a 6-2 stone at either end of the 6-6 stone and, as a bonus, may place another stone worth a total of 8 at right angles, like the 5-3 as shown here. The other player now has a chance to place a domino to match any of the free ends (6 or 2 or 3, in this example) as a first move, and may have a bonus move by playing a stone to equal any of the dominoes on the table (12 or 8 or the value of the domino just played, in this example). The bonus move is optional, and may be missed without penalty. However, a player who cannot make a first move by placing a stone on a free end must take one extra stone from the boneyard, to use immediately if possible or, if not, to keep for a future turn. The winner is the first player to run out of dominoes.

Record all the bonus moves from one game of Domino Bonus Game

30   Component Su Doku Puzzle

Teaching points

▶ Combining small components to create numbers up to 13.

▶ Splitting numbers into chunks, i.e. into components, or number bonds.

▶ The connection between addition, subtraction and missing addend problems.

▶ Logical reasoning.

Note to member of staff or parent

▶ The child should begin by answering the questions in the Tips section. Make sure the child thinks about the questions and is not simply copying the answers from a previous puzzle.

▶ The Tips section must be folded back so that the answers are hidden before the child starts to solve the puzzle.

▶ There must be no adding or subtracting by counting in ones, on fingers or otherwise.

▶ The child should use only logic. The puzzles in this book have been carefully designed so that the solver need never resort to guesswork or trial and error.

Equipment needed

A pencil and rubber.

30. Component Su Doku Puzzle

Name:

Date:

When to hand it in:

Instructions

Complete the Su Doku grid so that the numbers 3 to 7 appear in each column and each row. The rectangular boxes enclose two different components that add up to the number at the top left of the box.

Tips: Work out these facts first:

· Each row and each column must add up to _____ .

· The smallest possible number is _____ and must be made of _____ and _____ .

· The next smallest possible number is _____ and must be made of _____ and _____ .

· The largest possible number is _____ and must be made of _____ and _____ .

· The next largest possible number is _____ and must be made of _____ and _____ .

Component Su Doku Puzzle

Digits 3 to 7

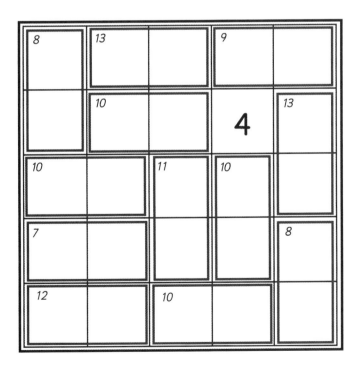

31 Difference Card War – a game for 2 players

Teaching points

▶ Mental subtraction of two numbers below 10.

▶ The word 'difference' used as a mathematical term to mean subtraction.

▶ Subtraction by complementary addition.

Note to member of staff or parent

▶ Make sure the child is using components knowledge or reasoning strategies to find the difference and accepts that counting in ones, on fingers or otherwise, is not allowed.

▶ Make sure that the focus is not on working backwards along an imagined number line or number track, but on working forwards in as few steps as possible. For example, to find the difference between 8 and 3, the child should not be thinking about mentally moving 3 steps backwards from 8, but should instead think about how much needs to be added to 3 to make 8. Rather than count on from 3, the child should be encouraged to derive the answer logically, perhaps from the knowledge that double 3 is 6, or by visualising the dot pattern of 8.

▶ The game and its variation should be played more than once and on more than one occasion.

▶ During one game, have the child use the blank space on the next page to record the game. The recording can be in any form the child chooses, provided it shows all the rounds of one game and includes the difference between the pairs as well as the value of the individual cards that were played.

▶ Once this game becomes too easy, cards with higher values can be introduced into the pack. One idea would be to use a full pack of playing cards and allocate the numbers 11, 12 and 13 to the Jacks, Queens and Kings. Another idea would be to write on laminated digit cards, altering all the 2s to read 12 and all the 1s to read any desired numbers between 11 and 19.

Equipment needed

A pack of cards made up of four each of the numbers 1 to 10 inclusive. If you have no digit cards, remove the appropriate cards from a standard pack of playing cards and treat the Aces as 1s.

31. Difference Card War

Name:

Date:

When to hand it in:

Instructions

Use a shuffled pack of cards made up of four each of the numbers 1 to 10 inclusive. Split the pack between two players. On each turn, both players pick up two cards from the top of their pack and announce the difference between the two card values. Whoever has the smaller difference wins all four cards. If both players' answers are the same, the four cards for that round are discarded. The winner is the player with most cards at the end of the game.

<u>Variation:</u> The greater difference wins all four cards in a round.

Record one game of Difference Card War

32   Component Su Doku Puzzle

Teaching points

▶ Combining small components to create numbers up to 13.

▶ Splitting numbers into chunks, i.e. into components, or number bonds.

▶ The connection between addition, subtraction and missing addend problems.

▶ Logical reasoning.

Note to member of staff or parent

▶ The child should begin by answering the questions in the Tips section. Make sure the child thinks about each question and is not simply copying the answers from a previous puzzle.

▶ The Tips section must be folded back so that the answers are hidden before the child starts to solve the puzzle.

▶ There must be no adding or subtracting by counting in ones, on fingers or otherwise.

▶ The child should use only logic. The puzzles in this book have been carefully designed so that the solver need never resort to guesswork or trial and error.

Equipment needed

A pencil and rubber.

32. Component Su Doku Puzzle

Name:

Date:

When to hand it in:

Instructions

Complete the Su Doku grid so that the numbers 3 to 7 appear in each column and each row. The rectangular boxes enclose two different components that add up to the number at the top left of the box.

Tips: Work out these facts first:

· Each row and each column must add up to _____ .

· The smallest possible number is _____ and must be made of _____ and _____ .

· The next smallest possible number is _____ and must be made of _____ and _____ .

· The largest possible number is _____ and must be made of _____ and _____ .

· The next largest possible number is _____ and must be made of _____ and _____ .

Component Su Doku Puzzle   Digits 3 to 7

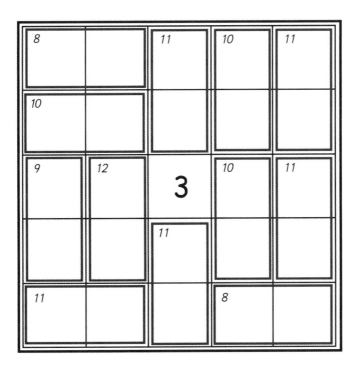

33   Cover the Number [Shut the Box] – a game for 2 players

Teaching points

▶ Repeated partitioning and recombining of the same small amounts.

▶ Mental addition and subtraction of two or more numbers up to a total of 12.

Note to member of staff or parent

▶ Make sure the child is recognising the dice patterns, not counting the dice spots.

▶ Make sure the child is using component knowledge, not counting in ones.

▶ When choosing which numbers to shade in, players have a free choice of any number of digits provided they are as yet unshaded on their board. For example, in response to a throw of 6, a player can (a) shade in the 6, or (b) shade the 1 and the 5, or (c) shade the 2 and the 4, or (d) shade the 1, the 2 and the 3.

▶ Note that, unlike most games, players do not take turns to throw the dice. In this game, one player keeps throwing the dice until there is nothing further to be done, before play passes to the next player.

▶ The game should be played more than once and on more than one occasion.

▶ Once the game is familiar, you can make the scoring more challenging by asking the child to add the numbers that remain unshaded on each player's board at the end of each round, instead of counting how many unshaded numbers remain.

▶ This is a paper and pencil version of the popular and traditional boxed game called 'Shut the Box' that is still widely available from toy shops.

Equipment needed

Two ordinary 6-sided spot dice. A pencil.

33. Cover the Number [Shut the Box]

Name:

Date:

When to hand it in:

Instructions

Throw both dice and announce the total. In one row of 1–9 digits on your board, shade in one, two or more numbers that total the same amount. Continue with the same row until you get stuck, i.e. you have no unshaded numbers left, or those that remain cannot be combined to match the latest dice throw. Your score is the number of digits left unshaded. Play now passes to the next player. The winner is the player with the lowest score after three rounds.

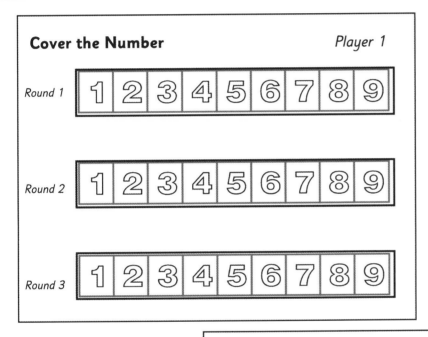

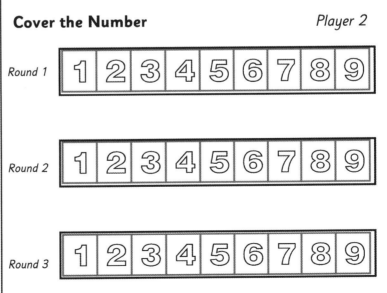

The Dyscalculia Resource Book © Ronit Bird, 2011 (SAGE)

34 Component Su Doku Puzzle

Teaching points

▶ Combining small components to create numbers up to 15.

▶ Splitting numbers into chunks, i.e. into components, or number bonds.

▶ The connection between addition, subtraction and missing addend problems.

▶ Logical reasoning.

Note to member of staff or parent

▶ The child should begin by answering the questions in the Tips section. Make sure the child thinks about each question and is not simply copying the answers from a previous puzzle.

▶ The Tips section must be folded back so that the answers are hidden before the child starts to solve the puzzle.

▶ There must be no adding or subtracting by counting in ones, on fingers or otherwise.

▶ The child should use only logic. The puzzles in this book have been carefully designed so that the solver need never resort to guesswork or trial and error.

Equipment needed

A pencil and rubber.

34. Component Su Doku Puzzle

Name:

Date:

When to hand it in:

Instructions
Complete the Su Doku grid so that the numbers 4 to 8 appear in each column and each row. The rectangular boxes enclose two different components that add up to the number at the top left of the box.

Tips: Work out these facts first:

· Each row and each column must add up to _____ .

· The smallest possible number is _____ and must be made of _____ and _____ .

· The next smallest possible number is _____ and must be made of _____ and _____ .

· The largest possible number is _____ and must be made of _____ and _____ .

· The next largest possible number is _____ and must be made of _____ and _____ .

Component Su Doku Puzzle   **Digits 4 to 8**

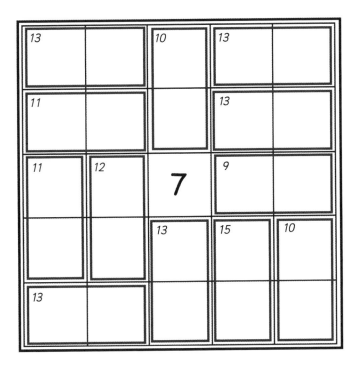

35 Triad Card & Domino Families – a game for 2 players

Teaching points

▶ Mental addition and subtraction of numbers up to 12.

▶ The connection between addition and subtraction.

▶ Informal and formal methods of recording a number relationship.

▶ Having to think carefully about what the +, − and = signs mean.

Note to member of staff or parent

▶ Make sure there is no counting in ones, on fingers or otherwise.

▶ Make sure the term 'triad' is understood as an arrangement of three numbers such that the number at the top is equal in value to the sum of the two numbers below.

▶ During one game, have the child use the blank space on the next page to record the game using the informal triad notation before recording the same information as formal equations, as set out in the instructions. The order of the numbers is not important, i.e. either $3 + 6 = 9$ or $6 + 3 = 9$ is equally acceptable if addition is called for, and either $9 - 3 = 6$ or $9 - 6 = 3$ is acceptable if subtraction is called for. However, you must insist that the child positions the number represented by the domino on its own on the far side of the equal sign, so that during a single game it is likely that some triads will need to be recorded as additions and others as subtractions.

▶ The game should be played more than once and on more than one occasion.

Equipment needed

A set of dominoes from 0-0 to 6-6. A pack of cards made up of four each of the numbers 1 to 10 inclusive. If you have no digit cards, remove the picture cards from a standard pack of playing cards and treat the Aces as 1s.

35. Triad Card & Domino Families

Name:

Date:

When to hand it in:

Instructions

Rules: For each round of the game, shuffle the cards and mix up the dominoes. Deal 8 cards and 4 dominoes face up to each player. Arrange as many of your numbers as possible in triad family groups, so that the two numbers at the bottom of the triad arrangement add up to the number at the top, the important constraint being that each triad must be composed of two cards and one domino. The domino may be in any position within the triad. E.g. in the example shown here, the two cards 9 and 6 are matched with a domino worth 3 and arranged into a triad family group. Each correct triad scores 1 point. Play three more rounds. The winner is the first to score 12 points, or the player with the highest score after 4 rounds of the game.

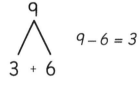

During the playing of any one game, record the families of facts from all four rounds, first informally using the triad notation, then formally as addition and subtraction equations. When writing the equation, position the number recording the total of the spots on the domino after the equal sign, i.e. follow this format: card plus or minus card = domino.

$$9$$
$$3 + 6 \qquad 9 - 6 = 3$$

Record one game of Triad Card & Domino Families

36 Component Su Doku Puzzle

Teaching points

▶ Combining small components to create numbers up to 15.

▶ Splitting numbers into chunks, i.e. into components, or number bonds.

▶ The connection between addition, subtraction and missing addend problems.

▶ Logical reasoning.

Note to member of staff or parent

▶ The child should begin by answering the questions in the Tips section. Make sure the child thinks about each question and is not simply copying the answers from a previous puzzle.

▶ The Tips section must be folded back so that the answers are hidden before the child starts to solve the puzzle.

▶ There must be no adding or subtracting by counting in ones, on fingers or otherwise.

▶ The child should use only logic. The puzzles in this book have been carefully designed so that the solver need never resort to guesswork or trial and error.

Equipment needed

A pencil and rubber.

36. Component Su Doku Puzzle

Name:

Date:

When to hand it in:

Instructions

Complete the Su Doku grid so that the numbers 4 to 8 appear in each column and each row. The rectangular boxes enclose two different components that add up to the number at the top left of the box.

Tips: Work out these facts first:

· Each row and each column must add up to _____ .

· The smallest possible number is _____ and must be made of _____ and _____ .

· The next smallest possible number is _____ and must be made of _____ and _____ .

· The largest possible number is _____ and must be made of _____ and _____ .

· The next largest possible number is _____ and must be made of _____ and _____ .

Component Su Doku Puzzle   Digits 4 to 8

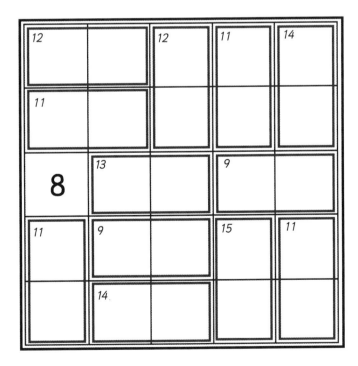

37   Prisoners – a game for 1 player

Teaching points

▶ Mental addition of pairs of numbers that total 11, 12 and 13.

Note to member of staff or parent

▶ Make sure the child accepts that adding in ones, on fingers or otherwise, is not allowed.

▶ As the pairs of cards are put together during play, both numbers and their total should be spoken aloud.

▶ The game should be played more than once and on more than one occasion.

Equipment needed

A standard pack of playing cards from which the Aces, 2s and 10s have been removed.

37. Prisoners

Name:

Date:

Instructions

Preparation: Use a pack of playing cards from which the Aces, 2s and 10s have been removed. Take out all the picture cards and arrange them face up at the top of your playing space. These cards represent the Prisoners, and can be arranged according to value (as shown below) or according to suit, whichever you prefer. In this game, a Jack is worth 11, a Queen is worth 12 and a King is worth 13. Shuffle the remaining 28 cards.

Rules: Deal 6 cards from the top of the pack and lay them face up. These cards are the active cards and, as soon as a pair of these cards is used, fill the empty gaps with two new cards from the pack. Your aim is to secure the release of the Prisoners by putting together any two of the active cards that add up to the same value as one of the picture cards. In other words, a Jack can be freed by two number cards with a total of 11, a Queen can be freed by a pair of cards totalling 12 and a King can be freed by a pair of cards totalling 13. As you play, name the two numbers being added and their total, and take all three cards out of play.

The game is won if all the Prisoners are liberated.

Prisoners   **A Solitaire Game**

38   Component Su Doku Puzzle

Teaching points

▶ Combining small components to create numbers up to 15.

▶ Splitting numbers into chunks, i.e. into components, or number bonds.

▶ The connection between addition, subtraction and missing addend problems.

▶ Logical reasoning.

Note to member of staff or parent

▶ The child should begin by answering the questions in the Tips section. Make sure the child thinks about each question and is not simply copying the answers from a previous puzzle.

▶ The Tips section must be folded back so that the answers are hidden before the child starts to solve the puzzle.

▶ There must be no adding or subtracting by counting in ones, on fingers or otherwise.

▶ The child should use only logic. The puzzles in this book have been carefully designed so that the solver need never resort to guesswork or trial and error.

Equipment needed

A pencil and rubber.

38. Component Su Doku Puzzle

Name:

Date:

When to hand it in:

Instructions

Complete the Su Doku grid so that the numbers 4 to 8 appear in each column and each row. The rectangular boxes enclose two different components that add up to the number at the top left of the box.

Tips: Work out these facts first:

· Each row and each column must add up to _____ .

· The smallest possible number is _____ and must be made of _____ and _____ .

· The next smallest possible number is _____ and must be made of _____ and _____ .

· The largest possible number is _____ and must be made of _____ and _____ .

· The next largest possible number is _____ and must be made of _____ and _____ .

Component Su Doku Puzzle

Digits 4 to 8

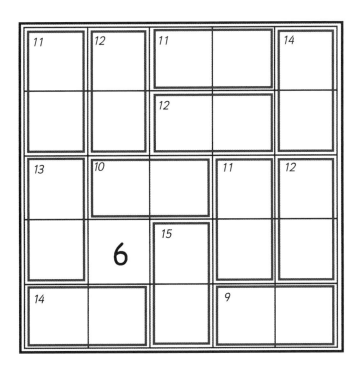

39 Cuisenaire Rods Staircase to 20 – a game for 2 players

Teaching points

▶ Complements to 20.

▶ Using diagrams of Cuisenaire rods as a transition between concrete and more abstract work.

Please note that children should not be asked to play this game unless they have had previous experience of working with the rods, including playing a concrete version of the game.

Note to member of staff or parent

▶ Make sure the child is familiar with Cuisenaire rods and can tell you all the colours and sizes in order: white, red, light green, purple, yellow, dark green, black, brown, blue, orange.

▶ Make sure that the child understands the term 'complement' to mean the number that completes another. In this game, the target number to complete is 20, rather than the more usual 10.

▶ Ask the child to tell you the 5 different complement to 10 facts (i.e. 9 + 1, 8 + 2, 7 + 3, 6 + 4 and 5 + 5) in any order. Make explicit the connection between these five facts and the facts being recorded during this game. For example, it is because we know that 2 and 8 are complements to 10 that we can deduce what must be added to 2 or 12 to make 20.

▶ The colouring of the rods on the game boards should be done lightly so that what is written on top will still be legible.

▶ Each player needs a pencil or pen with a distinctive colour so that the recorded complement facts can be attributed to the correct player for scoring purposes.

Equipment needed

A 1–10 die or two ordinary 6-sided dice on which the 6s are covered with a blank sticker, to represent zero. Two dark-coloured pens or pencils in different colours. 9 coloured pencils to match the Cuisenaire colours listed above. Please note that only 9 colours are needed because the smallest rod, white, is represented by an uncoloured square. In order to make recognition easier for the child, the purple should be a pinkish rather than a bluish purple, and the blue should be a dark blue.

39. Cuisenaire Rods Staircase to 20

Name:

Date:

When to hand it in:

Instructions

Lightly colour the game board below in the correct Cuisenaire colours. Take turns to throw a 1–10 die and find a step on the staircase where you can match the die throw to the relevant rod. Announce the complement of that number to 20. E.g. if you throw a 2, find the step representing 2 or 12 and say what must be added to make 20. Record the fact on the dotted line. If both facts are already recorded, you can do nothing on this turn. The winner is the first to record facts for three adjacent steps, i.e. complement facts for three consecutive numbers.

Cuisenaire Rods Staircase to 20

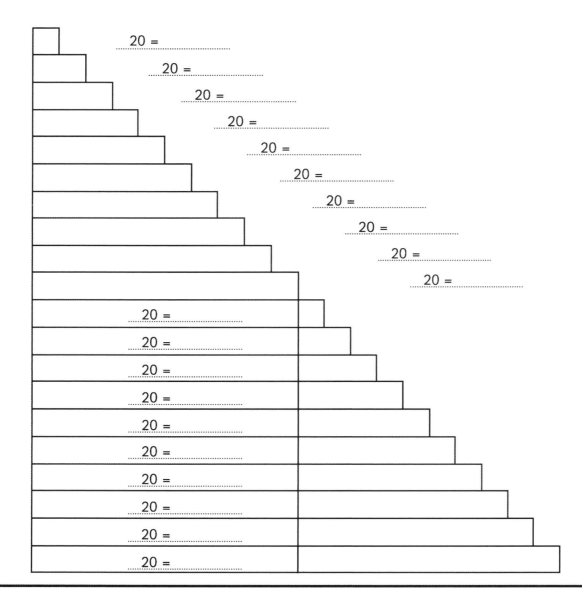

40 Component Su Doku Puzzle

Teaching points

▶ Combining small components to create numbers up to 15.

▶ Splitting numbers into chunks, i.e. into components, or number bonds.

▶ The connection between addition, subtraction and missing addend problems.

▶ Logical reasoning.

Note to member of staff or parent

▶ The child should begin by answering the questions in the Tips section. Make sure the child thinks about each question and is not simply copying the answers from a previous puzzle.

▶ The Tips section must be folded back so that the answers are hidden before the child starts to solve the puzzle.

▶ There must be no adding or subtracting by counting in ones, on fingers or otherwise.

▶ The child should use only logic. The puzzles in this book have been carefully designed so that the solver need never resort to guesswork or trial and error.

Equipment needed

A pencil and rubber.

40. Component Su Doku Puzzle

Name:

Date:

When to hand it in:

Instructions

Complete the Su Doku grid so that the numbers 4 to 8 appear in each column and each row. The rectangular boxes enclose two different components that add up to the number at the top left of the box.

Tips: Work out these facts first:

· Each row and each column must add up to _____ .

· The smallest possible number is _____ and must be made of _____ and _____ .

· The next smallest possible number is _____ and must be made of _____ and _____ .

· The largest possible number is _____ and must be made of _____ and _____ .

· The next largest possible number is _____ and must be made of _____ and _____ .

Component Su Doku Puzzle

Digits 4 to 8

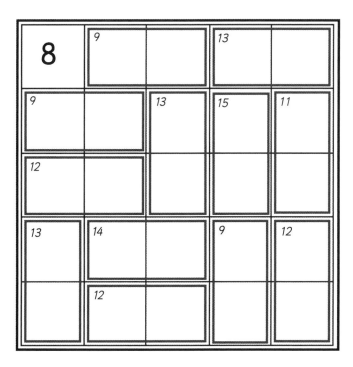

41 Component Su Doku Puzzle

Teaching points

▶ Practice in combining small components to create numbers up to 11.

▶ Practice in splitting numbers into chunks, i.e. into components.

▶ The connection between addition, subtraction and missing addend problems.

▶ Logical reasoning.

Note to member of staff or parent

▶ The child should begin by answering the questions in the Tips section. Make sure the child thinks about each question and is not simply copying the answers from a previous puzzle.

▶ The Tips section must be folded back so that the answers are hidden before the child starts to solve the puzzle.

▶ There must be no adding or subtracting by counting in ones, on fingers or otherwise.

▶ The child should use only logic. The puzzles in this book have been carefully designed so that the solver need never resort to guesswork or trial and error.

Equipment needed

A pencil and rubber.

41. Component Su Doku Puzzle

Name:

Date:

When to hand it in:

Instructions

Complete the Su Doku grid so that the numbers 1 to 6 appear once in each column and each row and also in each of the cells defined by the background shading. The rectangular boxes enclose two or three different components that add up to the number at the top left of the box.

Tips: Work out these facts first:

• Each row and each column must add up to _____ .

• The two smallest possible numbers are _____ (i.e. _____ + _____) and _____ (i.e. _____ + _____).

• The two largest possible numbers are _____ (i.e. _____ + _____) and _____ (i.e. _____ + _____).

• How can you create 6 from three different components? 6 = _____ + _____ + _____ .

• How can you create 7 from three different components? 7 = _____ + _____ + _____ .

Component Su Doku Puzzle

Digits 1 to 6

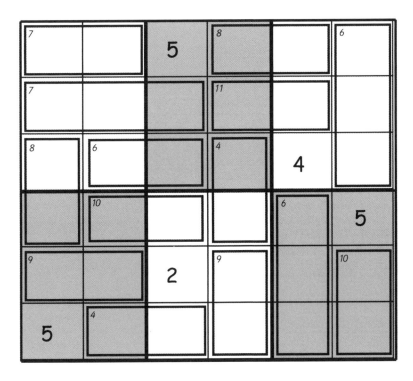

42   Component Su Doku Puzzle

Teaching points

▌ Combining small components to create numbers up to 17.

▌ Splitting numbers into chunks, i.e. into components, or number bonds.

▌ The connection between addition, subtraction and missing addend problems.

▌ Logical reasoning.

Note to member of staff or parent

▌ The child should begin by answering the questions in the Tips section.

▌ The Tips section must be folded back so that the answers are hidden before the child starts to solve the puzzle.

▌ There must be no adding or subtracting by counting in ones, on fingers or otherwise.

▌ The child should use only logic. The puzzles in this book have been carefully designed so that the solver need never resort to guesswork or trial and error.

Equipment needed

A pencil and rubber.

42. Component Su Doku Puzzle

Name:

Date:

When to hand it in:

Instructions

Complete the Su Doku grid so that the numbers 5 to 9 appear in each column and each row. The rectangular boxes enclose two different components that add up to the number at the top left of the box.

Tips: Work out these facts first:

· Each row and each column must add up to _____ .

· The two smallest possible numbers are _____ (i.e. _____ + _____) and _____ (i.e. _____ + _____).

· The two largest possible numbers are _____ (i.e. _____ + _____) and _____ (i.e. _____ + _____).

Component Su Doku Puzzle   **Digits 5 to 9**

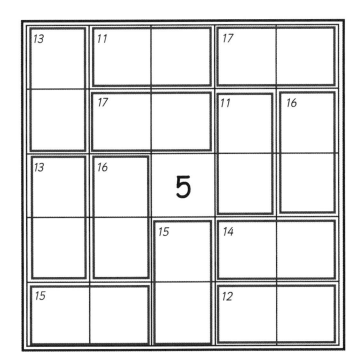

43   Difference Su Doku Puzzle

Teaching points

▶ Combining small components to create larger numbers and partitioning numbers back into components.

▶ The connection between addition, subtraction and missing addend problems.

▶ Logical reasoning.

Note to member of staff or parent

▶ There must be no adding or subtracting by counting in ones, on fingers or otherwise.

▶ The child should use only logic. The puzzles in this book have been carefully designed so that the solver need never resort to guesswork or trial and error.

Equipment needed

A pencil and rubber.

43. Difference Su Doku Puzzle

Name:

Date:

When to hand it in:

Instructions
Complete the Su Doku grid so that the numbers 1 to 5 appear once in each column and each row. Pairs of numbers are enclosed in rectangular boxes and the difference between the two enclosed numbers is shown at the top of each box.

Difference Su Doku Puzzle   **Digits 1 to 5**

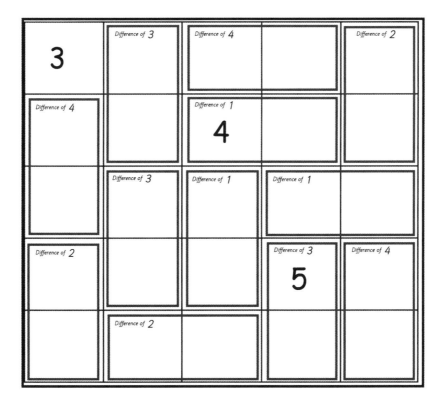

44 Component Su Doku Puzzle

Teaching points

▶ Combining small components to create numbers up to 17.

▶ Splitting numbers into chunks, i.e. into components, or number bonds.

▶ The connection between addition, subtraction and missing addend problems.

▶ Logical reasoning.

Note to member of staff or parent

▶ The child should begin by answering the questions in the Tips section.

▶ The Tips section must be folded back so that the answers are hidden before the child starts to solve the puzzle.

▶ There must be no adding or subtracting by counting in ones, on fingers or otherwise.

▶ The child should use only logic. The puzzles in this book have been carefully designed so that the solver need never resort to guesswork or trial and error.

Equipment needed

A pencil and rubber.

44. Component Su Doku Puzzle

Name:

Date:

When to hand it in:

Instructions

Complete the Su Doku grid so that the numbers 5 to 9 appear in each column and each row. The rectangular boxes enclose two different components that add up to the number at the top left of the box.

Tips: Work out these facts first:

· Each row and each column must add up to _____ .

· The two smallest possible numbers are _____ (i.e. _____ + _____) and _____ (i.e. _____ + _____).

· The two largest possible numbers are _____ (i.e. _____ + _____) and _____ (i.e. _____ + _____).

Component Su Doku Puzzle

Digits 5 to 9

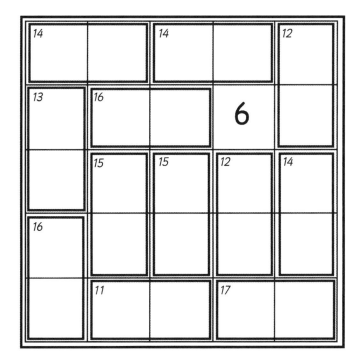

45   Component Su Doku Puzzle

Teaching points

▶ Practice in combining small components to create numbers up to 13.

▶ Practice in splitting numbers into chunks, i.e. into components.

▶ The connection between addition, subtraction and missing addend problems.

▶ Logical reasoning.

Note to member of staff or parent

▶ The child should begin by answering the questions in the Tips section.

▶ The Tips section must be folded back so that the answers are hidden before the child starts to solve the puzzle.

▶ There must be no adding or subtracting by counting in ones, on fingers or otherwise.

▶ The child should use only logic. The puzzles in this book have been carefully designed so that the solver need never resort to guesswork or trial and error.

Equipment needed

A pencil and rubber.

45. Component Su Doku Puzzle

Name:

Date:

When to hand it in:

Instructions

Complete the Su Doku grid so that the numbers 2 to 7 appear once in each column and each row and also in each of the cells defined by the background shading. The rectangular boxes enclose two different components that add up to the number at the top left of the box.

Tips: Work out these facts first:

· Each row and each column must add up to _____ .

· The two smallest possible numbers are _____ (i.e. _____ + _____) and _____ (i.e. _____ + _____).

· The two largest possible numbers are _____ (i.e. _____ + _____) and _____ (i.e. _____ + _____).

Component Su Doku Puzzle   Digits 2 to 7

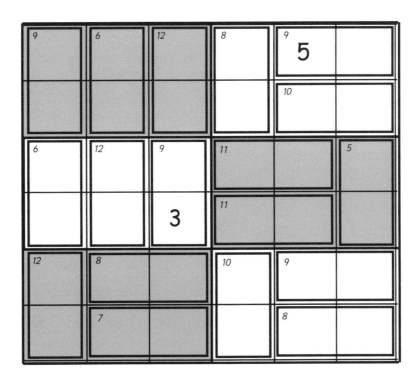

46   Component Su Doku Puzzle

Teaching points

▶ Combining small components to create numbers up to 17.

▶ Splitting numbers into chunks, i.e. into components, or number bonds.

▶ The connection between addition, subtraction and missing addend problems.

▶ Logical reasoning.

Note to member of staff or parent

▶ The child should begin by answering the questions in the Tips section.

▶ The Tips section must be folded back so that the answers are hidden before the child starts to solve the puzzle.

▶ There must be no adding or subtracting by counting in ones, on fingers or otherwise.

▶ The child should use only logic. The puzzles in this book have been carefully designed so that the solver need never resort to guesswork or trial and error.

Equipment needed

A pencil and rubber.

46. Component Su Doku Puzzle

Name:

Date:

When to hand it in:

Instructions

Complete the Su Doku grid so that the numbers 5 to 9 appear in each column and each row. The rectangular boxes enclose two different components that add up to the number at the top left of the box.

Tips: Work out these facts first:

· Each row and each column must add up to _____ .

· The two smallest possible numbers are _____ (i.e. _____ + _____) and _____ (i.e. _____ + _____).

· The two largest possible numbers are _____ (i.e. _____ + _____) and _____ (i.e. _____ + _____).

· Using only numbers 5 to 9, what three different numbers could be combined to create 18?

Component Su Doku Puzzle

Digits 5 to 9

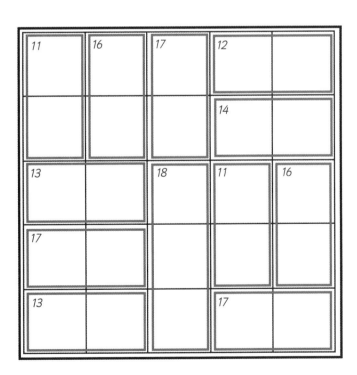

47   Difference Su Doku Puzzle

Teaching points

▌ Combining small components to create larger numbers and partitioning numbers back into components.

▌ The connection between addition, subtraction and missing addend problems.

▌ Logical reasoning.

Note to member of staff or parent

▌ There must be no adding or subtracting by counting in ones, on fingers or otherwise.

▌ The child should use only logic. The puzzles in this book have been carefully designed so that the solver need never resort to guesswork or trial and error.

Equipment needed

A pencil and rubber.

47. Difference Su Doku Puzzle

Name:

Date:

When to hand it in:

Instructions

Complete the Su Doku grid so that the numbers 1 to 5 appear once in each column and each row. Pairs of numbers are enclosed in rectangular boxes and the difference between the two enclosed numbers is shown at the top of each box.

Difference Su Doku Puzzle

Digits 1 to 5

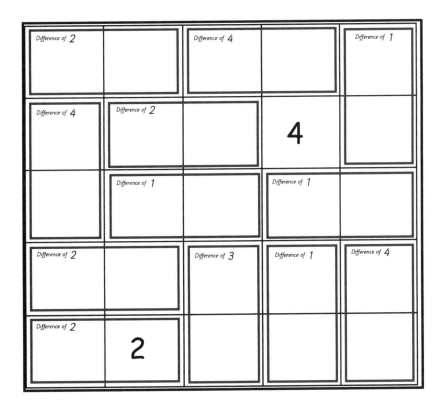

48   Component Su Doku Puzzle

Teaching points

▶ Combining small components to create numbers up to 17.

▶ Splitting numbers into chunks, i.e. into components, or number bonds.

▶ The connection between addition, subtraction and missing addend problems.

▶ Logical reasoning.

Note to member of staff or parent

▶ The child should begin by answering the questions in the Tips section.

▶ The Tips section must be folded back so that the answers are hidden before the child starts to solve the puzzle.

▶ There must be no adding or subtracting by counting in ones, on fingers or otherwise.

▶ The child should use only logic. The puzzles in this book have been carefully designed so that the solver need never resort to guesswork or trial and error.

Equipment needed

A pencil and rubber.

48. Component Su Doku Puzzle

Name:

Date:

When to hand it in:

Instructions

Complete the Su Doku grid so that the numbers 5 to 9 appear in each column and each row. The rectangular boxes, and an L-shape, enclose two or three different components that add up to the number at the top left of the box.

Tips: Work out these facts first:

· Each row and each column must add up to _____ .

· The two smallest possible numbers are _____ (i.e. _____ + _____) and _____ (i.e. _____ + _____).

· The two largest possible numbers are _____ (i.e. _____ + _____) and _____ (i.e. _____ + _____).

· Using only numbers 5 to 9, what three different numbers could be combined to create 18?

· Using only numbers 5 to 9, what three different numbers could be combined to create 24?

Component Su Doku Puzzle   **Digits 5 to 9**

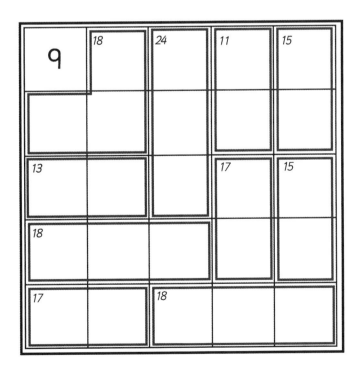

49   Component Su Doku Puzzle

Teaching points

▶ Practice in combining small components to create numbers up to 17.

▶ Practice in splitting numbers into chunks, i.e. into components.

▶ The connection between addition, subtraction and missing addend problems.

▶ Logical reasoning.

Note to member of staff or parent

▶ The child should begin by answering the questions in the Tips section. Make sure the child thinks about the questions and is not simply copying the answers from a previous puzzle.

▶ The Tips section must be folded back so that the answers are hidden before the child starts to solve the puzzle.

▶ There must be no adding or subtracting by counting in ones, on fingers or otherwise.

▶ The child should use only logic. The puzzles in this book have been carefully designed so that the solver need never resort to guesswork or trial and error.

Equipment needed

A pencil and rubber.

49. Component Su Doku Puzzle

Name:

Date:

When to hand it in:

Instructions

Complete the Su Doku grid so that the numbers 4 to 9 appear once in each column and each row and also in each of the cells defined by the background shading. The rectangular boxes enclose two different components that add up to the number at the top left of the box.

Tips: Work out these facts first:

· Each row and each column must add up to _____ .

· The two smallest possible numbers are _____ (i.e. _____ + _____) and _____ (i.e. _____ + _____).

· The two largest possible numbers are _____ (i.e. _____ + _____) and _____ (i.e. _____ + _____).

Component Su Doku Puzzle

Digits 4 to 9

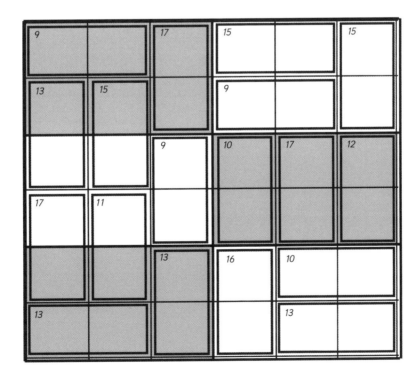

50   Standing Aces – a game for 1 player

Teaching points

▶ Mental addition of pairs of numbers totalling between 4 and 20.

Note to member of staff or parent

▶ Make sure that the child accepts that adding in ones, on fingers or otherwise, is not allowed.

▶ As pairs of cards are put together during play, the child should say both numbers and their total aloud.

▶ The game should be played more than once and on more than one occasion.

Equipment needed

A standard pack of playing cards from which the 10s, Kings and Queens have been removed.

50. Standing Aces

Name:

Date:

Instructions

Use a pack of playing cards from which the 10s, Kings and Queens have been removed. Count each Jack as 11. Shuffle the cards and lay out 16 cards face up in a 4 by 4 array.

Aces cannot be moved or used as part of any addition. Look for pairs of cards in the same suit. If, and only if, the two cards lie in the same row or column, you can clear away both the cards of the same suit by calculating and announcing the total value of the pair. As soon as spaces appear in the array, fill the gaps with two new cards from the pack.

The game is won when only the four Aces remain. However, since this is a difficult patience game to win, you should keep a record of how many cards you are left with each time you play and try to beat your own record in subsequent games.

Standing Aces   **A Solitaire Game**

PART II

Multiplication Tables and Division Games and Puzzles

51   Double & Half Dominoes – a game for 2 players

Teaching points

▶ The double and half facts of the even numbers up to 10, which are also key component facts, e.g. 4 and 4 are regarded as the key components of 8 because double 4 is 8.

▶ Doubling and halving are inverse operations.

Note to member of staff or parent

▶ Make sure the child is recognising the dice patterns, not counting the dice spots.

▶ Prepare a game board for a second player by sketching an outline of 10 blank dominoes, in two equal rows, on a piece of paper.

▶ Be sure to create the small circles empty during the preparation stage so that they can be shaded in during play.

▶ The figure below shows what the domino patterns for each of the numbers should look like, but note that on the game boards there will be two dominoes for each number and that each player has a free choice about the position and sequence of the numbers.

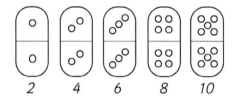

2   4   6   8   10

▶ Whatever the throw of the die, the matching pattern must be taken as a whole and cannot be split into smaller components, for example, a throw of 4 can only result in the shading of the circles on one half of a domino labelled with the number 8. If all four of the patterns of 4 on the board are already shaded, the player misses the turn.

▶ Both players must say out loud the related doubles and halves facts during play, for example, if the die throw is 4, say '4 is half of 8' or 'Half of 8 is 4', choose one of the dominoes labelled 8 and shade in one side of it while saying 'Double 4 is 8' or 'Two 4s are 8'.

Equipment needed

An ordinary 6-sided spot die. Paper and pencil.

51. Double & Half Dominoes

Name:

Date:

When to hand it in:

Instructions

Preparation: Each player creates a game board (one player using the board below) by labelling ten blank domino outlines with two each of the numbers 2, 4, 6, 8 and 10. Players have a free choice about the order and position of their numbers. On each side of each domino, players draw half of the labelled number in the form of a dice pattern, drawing small empty circles, not dots. So, a domino labelled '4' needs two small circles on either side of the central dividing line, a domino labelled '8' needs patterns of 4 on each side, as in the example shown here, etc.

Rules: Take turns to throw a die and throw again if you get a 6. Match the die throw to half of one of your labelled numbers and shade in the matching pattern, i.e. shade one side of one domino on each turn. Announce the half and double facts aloud. So, if you throw a 4, shade in the 4 circles on one side of one of the '8' dominoes and say: "Half of 8 is 4. Double 4 is 8". If all the matching patterns are already shaded, you can do nothing on this turn. The winner is the first to complete all five dominoes in either one of the rows on the game board.

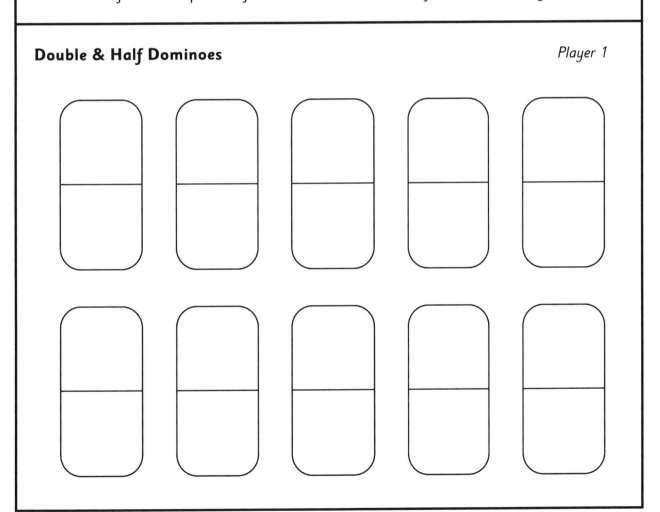

Double & Half Dominoes

Player 1

52   Cuisenaire Rods Pyramid – a game for 2 players

Teaching points

▶ Double all the numbers up to 10 + 10 and half the even numbers from 2 to 20.

▶ Each step of the doubles pyramid is 2 – not 1! – more or less than the step before.

▶ Recording double facts in a multiplicative way rather than as an addition.

▶ Visualising Cuisenaire rods as a way of moving away from concrete and towards diagrammatic representations in order to support mental calculation.

Please note that children should not be asked to play this game unless they have had previous experience of working with the rods, including playing a concrete version of the game.

Note to member of staff or parent

▶ Make sure that the child is familiar with Cuisenaire rods and can tell you all the colours and sizes in order: white, red, light green, purple, yellow, dark green, black, brown, blue, orange.

▶ Make sure the language used by both players focuses on the idea that doubling means 'twice as much/as many', rather than 'add one more'. The symmetrical pattern should help to emphasise this fact.

▶ No counting in ones is allowed, apart from the two 10-square rectangles at the base of the pyramid. The 5 + 5 fact is coloured in first, so that players can use this, together with the top and bottom steps of the pyramid, to navigate around the pyramid without counting, for example, if the pencil picked is brown, the player should either find the step two before the longest step, or three further than the yellow step, but is not allowed to count either 8 steps or 8 squares.

▶ The game should be repeated on different occasions until the child can visualise the pyramid sufficiently well to answer the same kind of questions mentally even when the doubling and halving questions are mixed and presented in a random order.

Equipment needed

Squared paper, preferably centimetre squared. Nine coloured pencils to match the colours listed above. Please note that only 9 colours are needed because the smallest rod is represented by a blank square. In order to make recognition easier for the child, the purple should be a pinkish rather than a bluish purple, and the blue should be a dark blue.

52. Cuisenaire Rods Pyramid

Name:

Date:

Instructions

Preparation: Use coloured pencils to colour the pyramid below in the Cuisenaire colours. Notice the fact that each step is *two* more or less than the previous step. It is *two* more or less because there is *one* more or less *on each side* of the pyramid. Visualising and remembering this will help you work out any doubles facts you don't know from the facts you do know.

Each player makes a game board by copying the outline of the pyramid onto squared paper. Start at the bottom and count ten squares to represent each orange rod. Do not count any of the subsequent steps, simply keep the line of symmetry in the middle and draw each step smaller by two squares — one on each side — as you complete the pyramid shape. Use the yellow pencil to colour the 5 + 5 step of both players' pyramids.

Rules: Put all the coloured pencils together and take turns to pick one at random, with your eyes closed. Lightly colour in the relevant step of the pyramid and announce the double and half facts for that step. The next time you pick the same colour (or the first time you pick the yellow pencil) you must write the double and half facts on the already-shaded step, e.g. write 'Double 5 = 10' and 'Half of 10 = 5' on the yellow step of the pyramid. If you pick the same colour yet again, you can do nothing on this turn. The winner is the first player with five adjacent steps — five steps all in a row — that are both coloured and labelled.

Cuisenaire Rods Pyramid

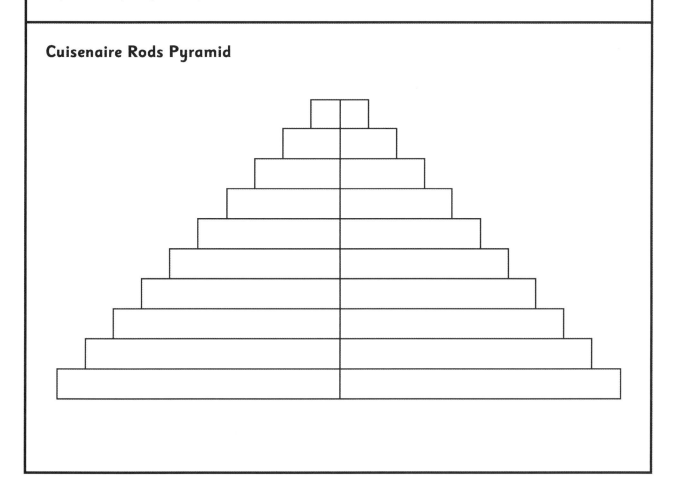

53   Butterfly Doubles [1–6] – a game for 2 players

Teaching points

▶ Doubling the numbers from 1 to 6.

▶ Halving the even numbers from 2 to 12.

▶ The number 1½ lies halfway between 1 and 2, and 2½ lies between 2 and 3, etc.

Note to member of staff or parent

▶ Make sure the child is not counting in ones, on fingers or otherwise.

▶ Make sure all the doubles are written inside the butterflies on both boards before the child begins to record any of the half values.

▶ When it comes to finding and recording half the doubled amounts and to finding the scores, encourage the child to take responsibility for both players' game boards.

Equipment needed

An ordinary 6-sided die. A pencil.

53. Butterfly Doubles [1–6]

Name:

Date:

When to hand it in:

Instructions

Take turns to throw a die. Write double the number inside a butterfly shape. After nine turns each, write under every butterfly what the original die throw must have been, i.e. find half of the recorded numbers. Your score is whichever of this second set of numbers occurs most frequently. So, score 4 if 4 appears most frequently under the butterflies. If two numbers occur with the same high frequencies, your score is the number halfway between them, e.g. as many 2s as 3s means you score 2½. The winner is the player with the higher score.

Butterfly Doubles   *Player 1*

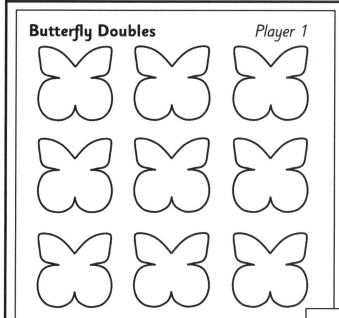

Butterfly Doubles   *Player 2*

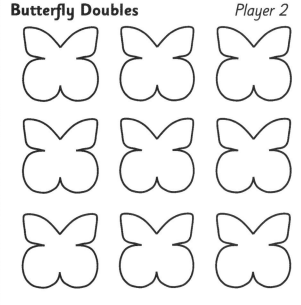

54   Halving Odd Multiples of Ten – a game for 1 player

Teaching points

▶ A partitioning method to make halving easier.

▶ Two useful informal notations: triads and arrows.

▶ Halving round numbers in which there are an odd number of tens.

▶ Reasoning routes to finding unknown facts from known facts.

Note to member of staff or parent

▶ Make sure the child is not simply following the instructions mechanically but can explain why the partitioning is a helpful step in preparation for halving.

▶ Make sure that every answer is covered up as soon as the child has finished recording it. Cover the example in the instructions section, too, once it has been understood.

▶ As soon as the informal recording is complete the child should repeat the question and answer out loud, for example, 'Half of 50 is 25'.

▶ The game should be repeated on different occasions until the child can visualise the technique sufficiently well to answer the same questions mentally.

▶ Although the arrows on the game board are designed to remind the child that halving is involved, when informally recording their own calculations children can draw simple arrows without any labelling, as shown below.

$$50$$
$$\diagdown\diagup$$
$$40 + 10 \qquad \text{or} \qquad 50 \; = 40 + 10$$
$$\downarrow \quad \downarrow \qquad\qquad\qquad \downarrow \quad \downarrow$$
$$20 + 5 \qquad\qquad\qquad\quad 20 \; + 5$$

▶ Once these six numbers are secure, alter the die to feature a new range of multiples of ten in which there are an odd number of tens.

Equipment needed

A 6-sided die on which these numbers appear: 30, 50, 70, 90, 110 and 130 (either write on a blank die or on stickers that cover the faces of an ordinary die). A pencil.

54. Halving Odd Multiples of Ten

Name:

Date:

When to hand it in:

Instructions

Use a die that has been altered to show these numbers: 30, 50, 70, 90, 110 and 130. Throw the die and copy the number into one of the boxes on the game board. Partition the number into the nearest even number of tens, plus the remaining (odd) ten, e.g. partition 50 into 40 plus 10. Halve each of the new numbers separately and record the answers using informal triad and arrow notations, as shown here. Combine the half amounts mentally to declare aloud what is half the number on the die. Hide the completed box so that you are not tempted to copy an answer when the same number is thrown again. After ten turns, your score is the die throw with the highest frequency. So, if 50 came up more often than any other number, your score is 50. If there is a tie for the highest frequency, your score is halfway between the numbers, e.g. as many 50s as 90s recorded at the top of your boxes results in a score of 70.

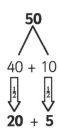

Play again to see how often you can score 90 or more. Keep playing until you can visualise the technique to find answers mentally. Next, play again with new numbers on the die.

Halving Odd Multiples of Ten

A Solitaire Game

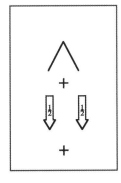 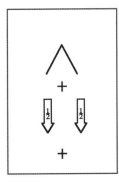 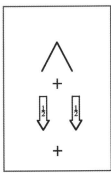 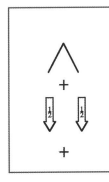 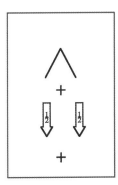

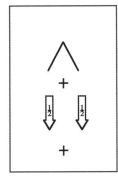 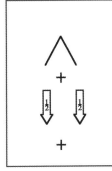 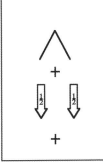 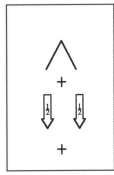 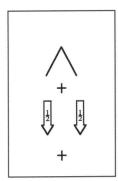

55 MAD [Multiplication and Division] Puzzles

Teaching points

▶ Easy times tables facts.

▶ Finding factors of given multiples up to 4×4.

▶ The connection between multiplication and division and between factors and products.

▶ Logical reasoning.

Note to member of staff or parent

▶ Make sure that the child begins by completing the practice multiplication grid, without any help or any opportunity to copy answers, in preparation for solving the puzzle.

▶ The completed practice grid must be hidden before the child starts to solve the puzzle. Warn the child in advance that it will not be available once it has been completed.

▶ Make sure that no calculation is attempted by counting in ones, on fingers or otherwise.

▶ Do not allow the child to chant a table from its beginning, e.g. $1\times$ ... $2\times$ ... $3\times$ ... etc.

▶ As the child works through the puzzle, any way of distinguishing between possible answers and final answers is acceptable, but a suggested method is to write the possibilities very lightly and very small and to rub out these digits once a conclusion has been reached.

▶ The child should use only logic. The puzzles in this book have been carefully designed so that the solver need never resort to guesswork or trial and error.

Equipment needed

A pencil and rubber.

55. MAD [Multiplication and Division] Puzzles

Name:

Date:

When to hand it in:

Instructions

Write the factors 1 to 4 in the circles so that each digit appears only once in each row and each column of each puzzle. The number shown at the top left of a rectangle enclosing two circles is the product of the two circled numbers, i.e. the result of multiplying them together.

Before you start: Prepare yourself by filling in the facts on this small multiplication grid, which is part of the familiar 10 x 10 multiplication square. (You need not fill in the square numbers, because the puzzle rules do not allow you to repeat a number in any row or column.)

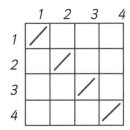

After completing the multiplication grid, fold it back to hide it from view before beginning on the puzzle.

MAD [Multiplication and Division] Puzzles
Digits 1 to 4

(a)

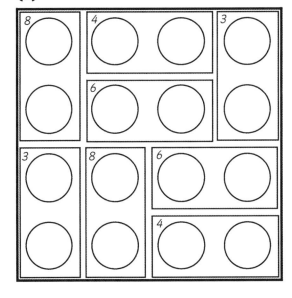

(b)

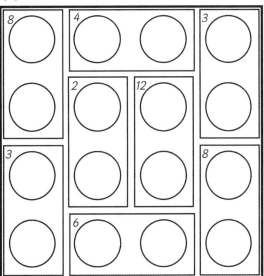

56 The 2 & 4 Times Tables Race – a game for 2 players

Teaching points

▶ The 2× and the 4× tables.

▶ The relationship between the two tables, i.e. that the answer to any step in the 4× table is double the same step of the 2× table.

▶ Using doubling to derive tables facts.

▶ Practice in deriving difficult tables facts by reasoning from key facts.

Please note that this game is designed for pupils who have already been taught how to reason about multiplication tables through concrete materials and who are now at the stage of using visualisation techniques in order to find answers mentally.

Note to member of staff or parent

▶ Make sure the child knows that the key facts of any table are the 2×, 5× and 10× steps (not necessarily in that order) and can confidently tell you the key facts of both these tables.

▶ Make sure the child is deriving answers from the key facts (e.g. 6×2 must be one step of 2 more than 5×2) or using doubling strategies (e.g. 6×2 is double 6 which is 12, so 6×4 must be double 12).

▶ Do not allow the child to count in ones or to chant a whole table starting from the beginning, e.g. 1× … 2× … 3× … etc.

▶ Make sure the child notices the relationship between the two tables as you play the game.

▶ On each turn, players must announce both possible answers aloud, even though only one of the answers can be covered by a counter during the turn.

▶ The game should be played more than twice – once on each board – and on more than one occasion.

Equipment needed

Two ordinary 6-sided dice on which the 6s are covered with a blank sticker, to represent zero. Counters, preferably semi-transparent, that fit on the squares of the game boards.

56. The 2 & 4 Times Tables Race

Name:

Date:

Instructions

On two dice, cover the 6s with blank stickers. Choose a board. Take turns to throw both dice and throw again if both show a blank. The total of both dice is the number you must now multiply by 2 and by 4. So, if the total amount on both dice is 6, announce that 6 x 2 = 12 and 6 x 4 = 24. Place a counter on either one of these answers. If both products (i.e. answers) are already covered, you can do nothing on this turn. The winner is the first player to place four counters in a row, horizontally, vertically or diagonally. Swap boards and play again.

The 2 x and 4 x Tables *Player 1*

24	16	6	20
4	20	14	32
10	8	40	18
36	2	28	12

The 2 x and 4 x Tables *Player 2*

12	32	16	28
14	4	36	6
2	18	10	20
20	24	8	40

The Dyscalculia Resource Book © Ronit Bird, 2011 (SAGE)

57   Five is Half of Ten – a game for 2 players

Teaching points

▶ The connection between the 5× and the 10× tables.

▶ A shortcut for finding 5 times a number is to halve 10 times that number.

▶ Using the area model of multiplication and division to support mental calculation.

Please note that this game is designed for pupils who have already had experience of creating rectangles and arrays out of concrete materials and who are now ready to use visualisation techniques as a way of working in a more abstract manner.

Note to member of staff or parents

▶ Make sure the child knows how to 'read' a rectangle as a representation of a multiplication or division fact, for example, the rectangle shown below can be read as $2 \times 10 = 20$ and as $10 \times 2 = 20$ and as $20 \div 2 = 10$ and as $20 \div 10 = 2$.

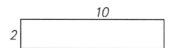

▶ During the pre-game practice, encourage the child to use the relevant rectangle sketch to support what is said aloud. For example, when reading the number 6 point to the side of the rectangle in the middle of the board that measures 6, when reading the number 10 point to the side that measures 10 on the same rectangle, when announcing that the product is 60 indicate the whole surface of the rectangle that measures 6 by 10 and when announcing that 5×6 is 30 indicate the surface of half the rectangle on one side of the dotted line.

▶ When preparing a second board for an opponent, or in order to play the game more than once, sketch the rectangles approximately without worrying unduly whether they are exactly to scale.

Equipment needed

A 1–10 die. If you do not have one, use two ordinary dice on which the 6s are covered with a blank sticker and throw again if both dice show blanks. Paper and pencil.

57. Five is Half of Ten

Name:

Date:

When to hand it in:

Instructions

Preparation: Practise all the facts orally and in a random order. E.g. throw a 1–10 die and if you throw a 6 say: "10 times 6 is 60, so 5 x 6 must be half of 60, which is 30. So, 5 x 6 is 30." Use the rectangles on the game board to support what you say, i.e. as you say the number 6 point to the side of the rectangle that measures 6, etc. Sketch another set of rectangles on paper, just like the game board below, for a second player.

Rules: Take turns to throw a 1–10 die and to announce the 10x and 5x facts about the number thrown. Write both facts inside the relevant rectangle on your board. If you throw the same number again, you can do nothing on this turn. If you throw a 1, have another turn. The winner is the first player with three rectangles in a row – horizontally, vertically or diagonally – in which the correct 10x and 5x facts have been written.

5 is Half of 10

Player 1

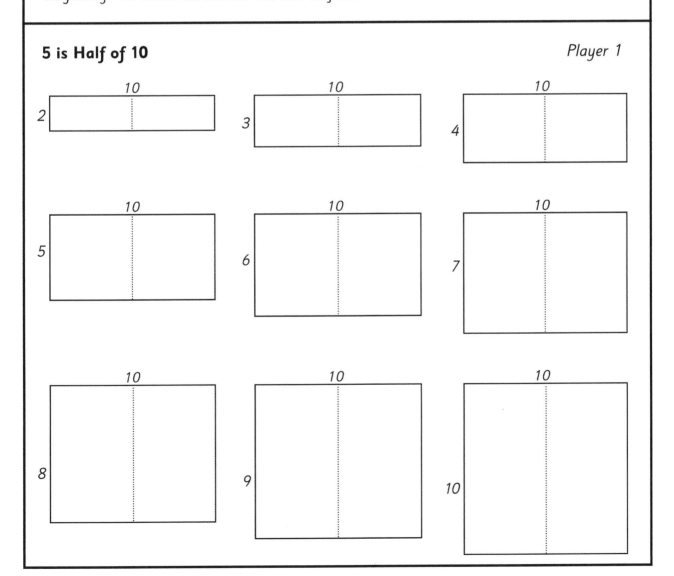

58 The 3x Table Coin Solitaire – a game for 1 player

Teaching points

▶ The 3× table.

▶ Using the step counting model of multiplication tables. Step counting in 3s.

▶ The commutative property of multiplication.

▶ Matching products to multiplication questions, without using the word 'division'.

▶ Practice in deriving the harder tables facts from the known key facts.

Please note that both the practice exercise and the game have been designed for pupils who have been taught how to reason about multiplication tables through concrete materials and who are now ready to use visualisation techniques in order to find answers mentally.

Note to member of staff or parent

▶ Make sure the child knows that the key facts of any table are the 2×, 5× and 10× steps (not necessarily in that order) and can confidently tell you the key facts for this table.

▶ During the preparation for the game, i.e. the labelling of the coins, encourage the child to step count (in 3s, not 1s) from 1 × 3. However, while playing the game the child is not allowed to recite the whole table from the beginning, nor to count in ones.

▶ The pre-game practice exercise is to make sure that the child knows how to derive all the necessary facts from the key facts in as few steps of reasoning as possible. For example, to find the answer to 8 × 3 from the key fact 5 × 3, it is better to add the three extra groups of 3 as a whole chunk, leading to the calculation 15 + 9, rather than step count three separate steps forward from 15.

▶ During the game, which is essentially a division exercise, the process outlined in the pre-game practice must be inverted. The first step is to find where a product lies in relation to the key facts before calculating how many steps away it is from the nearest key fact.

▶ The game should be played more than once and on more than one occasion. On each occasion the coins should be labelled afresh by the child.

Equipment needed

10 small coins. Round sticky labels of a size to fit on the coins. Also, a 1–10 die or some other way of generating the numbers from 1 to 10 in a random order, for the pre-game practice.

58. The 3x Table Coin Solitaire

Name:

Date:

Instructions

Practice: Practise deriving all the steps of the 3x table from the key facts, like this:
- 5x is half of 10x
- 2x and 4x (and 8x, if you like) are found by doubling and redoubling
- 9x is one step less than 10x
- 3x and 6x are one step more than a key fact
- 7x and 8x are 2 or 3 steps more than a key fact.

Use a 1–10 die, or a shuffled stack of digit cards showing numbers from 1 to 10, to help you practise finding all the steps of this multiplication table in a random order.

Preparation: Attach stickers to one side of 10 small coins. Write the multiples from the 3x tables (i.e. the answers to the questions on the game board below) on the stickers, one product to each coin. Turn the coins over and mix them.

Rules: Pick up a coin, and place it on top of the matching pair of questions (or on top of the single question if the multiple is a square number). When there are only two coins remaining, slide one under the bottom corner of the page and try to predict what number is on the hidden coin. Play on to find if you guessed right.

You should be able to win roughly half the games you play.

The 3x Table Coin Solitaire

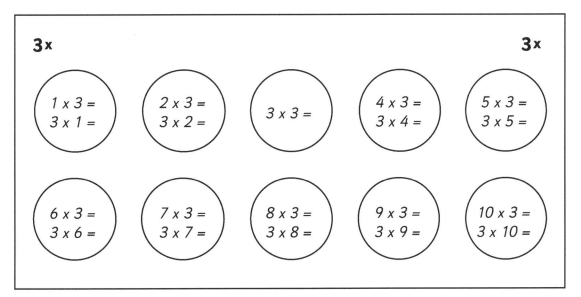

3x   **3x**

1 x 3 =
3 x 1 =

2 x 3 =
3 x 2 =

3 x 3 =

4 x 3 =
3 x 4 =

5 x 3 =
3 x 5 =

6 x 3 =
3 x 6 =

7 x 3 =
3 x 7 =

8 x 3 =
3 x 8 =

9 x 3 =
3 x 9 =

10 x 3 =
3 x 10 =

Hiding place for the final coin

59   MAD [Multiplication and Division] Puzzles

Teaching points

▶ Easy times tables facts.

▶ Finding factors of given multiples up to 5×5.

▶ The connection between multiplication and division and between factors and products.

▶ Logical reasoning.

Note to member of staff or parent

▶ Make sure that the child begins by completing the practice multiplication grid, without any help or any opportunity to copy answers, in preparation for solving the puzzle.

▶ The completed practice grid must be hidden before the child starts to solve the puzzle. Warn the child in advance that it will not be available once it has been completed.

▶ Make sure that no calculation is attempted by counting in ones, on fingers or otherwise.

▶ Do not allow the child to chant a table from its beginning, e.g. 1× ... 2× ... 3× ... etc.

▶ As the child works through the puzzle, any way of distinguishing between possible answers and final answers is acceptable, but a suggested method is to write the possibilities very lightly and very small and to rub out these digits once a conclusion has been reached.

▶ The child should use only logic. The puzzles in this book have been carefully designed so that the solver need never resort to guesswork or trial and error.

Equipment needed

A pencil and rubber.

59. MAD [Multiplication and Division] Puzzles

Name:

Date:

When to hand it in:

Instructions

Write the factors 1 to 4 in the circles of the first puzzle (a) and 2 to 5 in the circles of the second puzzle (b) so that each digit appears only once in each row and each column. The product of two numbers is shown at the top left of each rectangle enclosing two circles.

Before you start: Prepare yourself by filling in the facts on this small multiplication grid, which is part of the familiar 10 x 10 multiplication square. (You need not fill in the square numbers, because the puzzle rules do not allow you to repeat a number in any row or column.)

After completing the multiplication grid, fold it back to hide it from view before beginning on the puzzle.

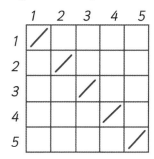

MAD [Multiplication and Division] Puzzles

(a) Digits 1 to 4

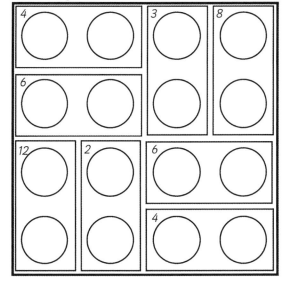

(b) Digits 2 to 5

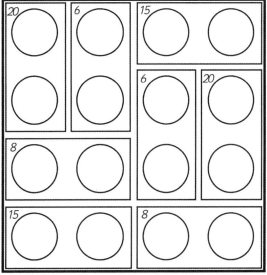

60   Key Multiples Bingo – a game for 2 players

Teaching points

▶ The key facts of a multiplication table are the 2×, 5× and 10× steps of the table.

▶ Some numbers are key facts of more than one multiplication table.

▶ The meaning of the term 'multiple'.

Please note that this game is designed for pupils who have already been taught about the key facts of multiplication tables through concrete materials and who are now at the stage of using visualisation techniques in order to find answers mentally.

Note to member of staff or parent

▶ Make sure the child knows that the key facts of any table are the 2×, 5× and 10× steps.

▶ Make sure the child knows how to find 2× a number by doubling and 10× a number by understanding place value. The 5× step is best derived by halving the 10× step.

▶ Do not allow the child to count in ones or to chant a whole table starting from the beginning.

▶ On each turn, players must announce all three key facts aloud, even though only one of the answers can be covered by a counter during the turn.

▶ The game should be played more than twice – once on each board – and on more than one occasion.

Equipment needed

A 1–10 die. If you do not have one, use two ordinary 6-sided dice on which the 6s are covered with a blank sticker, to represent zero. Counters, preferably semi-transparent, that fit on the squares of the game boards.

60. Key Multiples Bingo

Name:

Date:

Instructions

Choose one of the boards below. Take turns to throw a 10-sided die. Throw again if you get a 1 and miss a turn if you get a 10 or a 0. Announce the three key facts for the relevant table, e.g. if you throw a 6, tell your opponent what are 2 x 6, 5 x 6 and 10 x 6. Place a counter on any one of these three multiples. If all three key facts are already covered, you may place a counter on the middle square, but once this square is covered you will have to miss any turn in which the same situation arises. The winner is the first player to place five counters in a row, horizontally, vertically or diagonally. Swap boards and play again.

Key Multiples Bingo   *Player 1*

15	30	20	12	70
10	4	18	40	50
40	16		90	25
60	12	8	35	30
45	6	10	14	80

Key Multiples Bingo   *Player 2*

60	10	70	30	6
12	90	15	16	50
8	14		45	80
40	30	20	4	10
18	25	12	40	35

61   MAD Puzzle

Teaching points

▶ Easy times tables facts.

▶ Finding factors of given multiples up to 5×5.

▶ The connection between multiplication and division and between factors and products.

▶ Logical reasoning.

Note to member of staff or parent

▶ Make sure that the child begins by completing the practice multiplication grid, without any help or any opportunity to copy answers, in preparation for solving the puzzle.

▶ The completed practice grid must be hidden before the child starts to solve the puzzle. Warn the child in advance that it will not be available once it has been completed.

▶ Make sure that no calculation is attempted by counting in ones, on fingers or otherwise.

▶ As the child works through the puzzle, any way of distinguishing between possible answers and final answers is acceptable, but a suggested method is to write the possibilities very lightly and very small and to rub out these digits once a conclusion has been reached.

▶ The child should use only logic. The puzzles in this book have been carefully designed so that the solver need never resort to guesswork or trial and error.

Equipment needed

A pencil and rubber.

61. MAD Puzzle

Name:

Date:

When to hand it in:

Instructions

Write the factors 1 to 5 in the circles so that each digit appears only once in each row and each column. The number shown at the top left of a rectangle enclosing two circles is the product of the two circled numbers, i.e. the result of multiplying them together.

Before you start: Prepare yourself by filling in the facts on this small multiplication grid, which is part of the familiar 10 x 10 multiplication square. (You need not fill in the square numbers, because the puzzle rules do not allow you to repeat a number in any row or column.)

After completing the multiplication grid, fold it back to hide it from view before beginning on the puzzle.

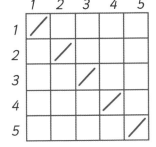

MAD Puzzle [MAD = Multiplication and Division]   Digits 1 to 5

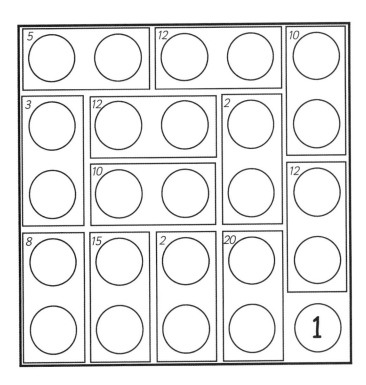

The Dyscalculia Resource Book © Ronit Bird, 2011 (SAGE)

62   Nines All-in-a-Row [9 is 1 less than 10] – a game for 2 players

Teaching points

▶ Finding 9 times a number working from 10 times that number.

▶ Using the area model of multiplication and division to support mental calculation.

Please note that this game is designed for pupils who have already had experience of creating rectangles and arrays out of concrete materials and who are now ready to use visualisation techniques as a way of working in a more abstract manner.

Note to member of staff or parents

▶ Make sure the child knows how to 'read' a rectangle as a representation of a multiplication or division fact, for example, a rectangle that is 2 units by 10 units can be read as: $2 \times 10 = 20$ and as $10 \times 2 = 20$ and as $20 \div 2 = 10$ and as $20 \div 10 = 2$.

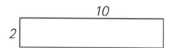

▶ Make sure the child knows how to derive the 9× step of any table from the 10× step. Ignore any other way of finding the 9× step or the 9× table facts for the purpose of this game, which is designed to practise the particular strategy of working back from 10.

▶ No counting back is allowed. So, to find 6 less than 60, say, the child must reason that the answer will be 50-something, the 'something' being the complement of 6, which is 4.

▶ During the pre-game practice, encourage the child to use the relevant rectangle sketch to support what is being said. So, for a die throw of 6 point to the side of the rectangle in the middle of the board that measures 6, when saying the number 10 point to the side that measures 10 on the same rectangle, when announcing the product 60 indicate the whole surface of the rectangle that measures 6 by 10, etc.

▶ When preparing a second board for an opponent, or in order to play the game more than once, sketch the rectangles approximately without worrying unduly whether they are exactly to scale.

Equipment needed

A 1–10 die. If you do not have one, use two ordinary dice on which the 6s are covered with a blank sticker and throw again if both dice show blanks. Paper and pencil.

62. Nines All-in-a-Row [9 is 1 less than 10]

Name:

Date:

When to hand it in:

Instructions

Preparation: Practise all the facts orally and in a random order. E.g. throw a 1–10 die and if you throw a 6 say: "10 sixes are 60, so 9 sixes must be six less than 60. So, 9 x 6 = 54." Prepare another set of rectangles, just like the game board below, for a second player.

Rules: Take turns to throw a 1–10 die and to announce the 10x and 9x facts about the number thrown. Write the 9x fact inside the relevant rectangle on your board. If you throw the same number again, you can do nothing on this turn. If you throw a 1, have another turn. The winner is the first player with three rectangles all in a row – horizontally, vertically or diagonally – in which the correct 9x facts have been written.

Nines All-in-a-Row [9 is 1 less than 10]   *Player 1*

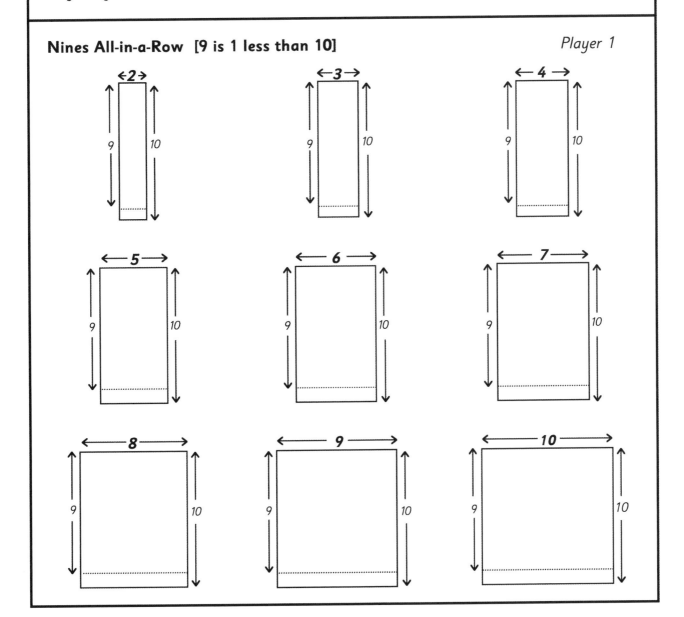

63   MAD Puzzle

Teaching points

◗ Times tables facts up to 5×5.

◗ Finding factors of given multiples.

◗ The connection between multiplication and division and between factors and products.

◗ Logical reasoning.

Note to member of staff or parent

◗ Make sure that the child begins by completing the practice multiplication grid, without any help or any opportunity to copy answers, in preparation for solving the puzzle.

◗ The completed practice grid must be hidden before the child starts to solve the puzzle. Warn the child in advance that it will not be available once it has been completed.

◗ Make sure that no calculation is attempted by counting in ones, on fingers or otherwise.

◗ As the child works through the puzzle, any way of distinguishing between possible answers and final answers is acceptable, but a suggested method is to write the possibilities very lightly and very small and to rub out these digits once a conclusion has been reached.

◗ The child should use only logic. The puzzles in this book have been carefully designed so that the solver need never resort to guesswork or trial and error.

Equipment needed

A pencil and rubber.

63. MAD Puzzle

Name:

Date:

When to hand it in:

Instructions

Write the factors 1 to 5 in the circles so that each digit appears only once in each row and each column. The number shown at the top left of a rectangle enclosing two circles is the product of the two circled numbers, i.e. the result of multiplying them together.

Before you start: Prepare yourself by filling in the facts on this small multiplication grid, which is part of the familiar 10 x 10 multiplication square. (You need not fill in the square numbers, because the puzzle rules do not allow you to repeat a number in any row or column.)

After completing the multiplication grid, fold it back to hide it from view before beginning on the puzzle.

MAD Puzzle

Digits 1 to 5

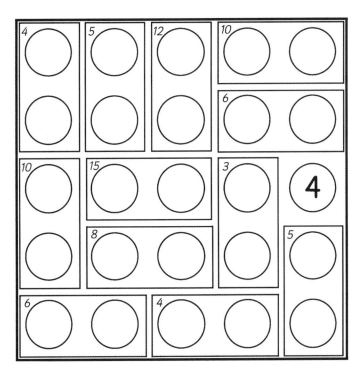

64   The 9x Table Coin Solitaire – a game for 1 player

Teaching points

▮ The 9× table.

▮ Using the step counting model of multiplication tables. Step counting in 9s.

▮ The commutative property of multiplication.

▮ Matching products to multiplication questions, without using the word 'division'.

▮ Practice in deriving the harder tables facts from the known key facts.

Please note that both the practice exercise and the game have been designed for pupils who have been taught how to reason about multiplication tables through concrete materials and who are now ready to use visualisation techniques in order to find answers mentally.

Note to member of staff or parent

▮ Make sure the child knows that the key facts of any table are the 2×, 5× and 10× steps (not necessarily in that order) and can confidently tell you the key facts for this table.

▮ During the preparation for the game, i.e. the labelling of the coins, encourage the child to step count (in 9s, not 1s) from 1 × 9. However, while playing the game the child is not allowed to recite the whole table from the beginning, nor to count in ones.

▮ The pre-game practice exercise is to make sure that the child knows how to derive all the necessary facts from the key facts in as few steps of reasoning as possible. For example, the child may choose to work from the key facts, as outlined in the 'Practice' section on the next page, or may realise that a quicker way to find an answer might be to recognise that 9× any number is one step less than 10× the same number.

▮ During the game, which is essentially a division exercise, the process outlined in the pre-game practice must be inverted. The first step is to find where a product lies in relation to the key facts before calculating how many steps away it is from the nearest key fact.

▮ The game should be played more than once and on more than one occasion. On each occasion the coins should be labelled afresh by the child.

Equipment needed

10 small coins. Round sticky labels of a size to fit on the coins. Also, a 1–10 die or some other way of generating the numbers from 1 to 10 in a random order, for the pre-game practice.

64. The 9x Table Coin Solitaire

Name:

Date:

Instructions

Practice: Practise deriving all the steps of the 9x table from the key facts, like this:
- 5x is half of 10x
- 2x and 4x (and 8x, if you like) are found by doubling and redoubling
- 9x is one step less than 10x
- 3x and 6x are one step more than a key fact
- 7x and 8x are 2 or 3 steps more than a key fact.

Use a 1–10 die, or a shuffled stack of digit cards showing numbers from 1 to 10, to help you practise finding all the steps of this multiplication table in a random order.

Preparation: Attach stickers to one side of 10 small coins. Write the multiples from the 9x tables (i.e. the answers to the questions on the game board below) on the stickers, one product to each coin. Turn the coins over and mix them.

Rules: Pick up a coin, and place it on top of the matching pair of questions (or on top of the single question if the multiple is a square number). When there are only two coins remaining, slide one under the bottom corner of the page and try to predict what number is on the hidden coin. Play on to find if you guessed right.

You should be able to win roughly half the games you play.

The 9x Table Coin Solitaire

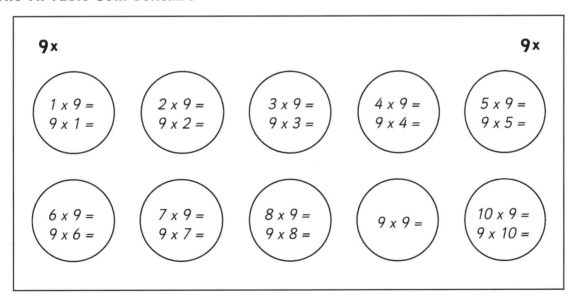

65 MAD Puzzle

Teaching points

▌ Times tables facts up to 5×5.

▌ Finding factors of given multiples.

▌ The connection between multiplication and division and between factors and products.

▌ Logical reasoning.

Note to member of staff or parent

▌ Make sure that the child begins by completing the practice multiplication grid, without any help or any opportunity to copy answers, in preparation for solving the puzzle.

▌ The completed practice grid must be hidden before the child starts to solve the puzzle. Warn the child in advance that it will not be available once it has been completed.

▌ Make sure that no calculation is attempted by counting in ones, on fingers or otherwise.

▌ As the child works through the puzzle, any way of distinguishing between possible answers and final answers is acceptable, but a suggested method is to write the possibilities very lightly and very small and to rub out these digits once a conclusion has been reached.

▌ The child should use only logic. The puzzles in this book have been carefully designed so that the solver need never resort to guesswork or trial and error.

Equipment needed

A pencil and rubber.

65. MAD Puzzle

Name:

Date:

When to hand it in:

Instructions

Write the factors 1 to 5 in the circles so that each digit appears only once in every horizontal row and no number is repeated in any vertical column. The number shown at the top left of a rectangle enclosing two circles is the product of the two circled numbers.

Before you start: Prepare yourself by filling in the facts on this small multiplication grid, which is part of the familiar 10 x 10 multiplication square. (You need not fill in the square numbers, because the puzzle rules do not allow you to repeat a number in any row or column.)

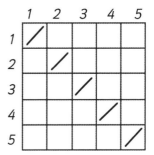

After completing the multiplication grid, fold it back to hide it from view before beginning on the puzzle.

MAD Puzzle   **Digits 1 to 5**

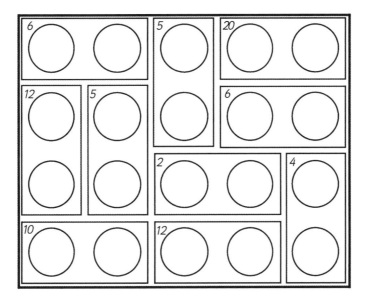

66 Don't Walk if You Can Take the Bus! – games for 2 players

Teaching points

▶ The 3× and the 6× tables (but the same game can be adapted for any table).

▶ Using the step counting model of multiplication tables. Step counting in 3s and 6s.

▶ Practice in deriving any tables fact from the key facts.

▶ A built-in incentive to derive new facts from key facts in as few steps as possible.

Note to member of staff or parents

▶ Make sure the child knows that the key facts of any table are the 2×, 5× and 10× steps (not necessarily in that order) and can confidently tell you the key facts for both the 3× and the 6× tables.

▶ No calculation is allowed by counting in ones, on fingers or otherwise.

▶ Make sure the child knows how to derive all the necessary facts from the key facts in as few steps of reasoning as possible. For example, for the 9× step of any table, the quickest way to find the answer is to know that it is one step less than 10× the same number.

▶ Note that the two game boards are to be used separately, with both opponents playing on the same game board and sharing a single pawn. Use the upper board on the next page to practise the 3× table and the lower board to practise the 6× table.

▶ The pawn stands on the lines designated by the arrows, not in the spaces.

▶ As the pawn is moved across the board, the players must announce the answer to every multiplication question related to each line that the pawn stands upon during the turn, and must talk aloud about how the movements relate to the times table, for example, if moving the pawn to 9×3, take it to the 10 bus-stop and say, '$10 \times 3 = 30$', before moving it back one section of track, continuing, 'So 9×3 must be 3 less than 30, which is 27'.

▶ Draw new game boards to practise any multiplication table that has already been taught but that needs reinforcing. It might be particularly useful to play a game with the 9× table next, since 9 is related to 3 and 6. For tables above the 6× table you might prefer to write digits on the game board instead of drawing dot patterns.

Equipment needed

A 1–10 die. If you do not have one, use two ordinary dice on which the 6s are covered with a blank sticker and throw again if both dice show blanks. A pawn. 20 coins.

66. Don't Walk if You Can Take the Bus!

Name:

Date:

Instructions

Rules: Both players use the same board and the same pawn, which is returned to the start position for each player's new turn. In complete contrast to real life, the pawn can move for free between any bus stops but must pay to walk from a bus stop to another destination.

Players take turns to throw the 1–10 die and move the pawn from the start position to the line matching the throw of the die, announcing each relevant times table fact that arises during the turn. Each player starts with 10 coins and must pay one coin for every section of track, i.e. each area containing one dot pattern, that the pawn is walked across. So, if the die throw is 9, it costs only one coin (and two times table answers) to get the pawn to the 9x line by walking back one stretch of track from the 10 bus-stop, but four coins (and five times table answers) to walk on from the 5 bus-stop. Step counting is allowed; counting in ones is not. Continue playing until one player loses by being the first to run out of coins.

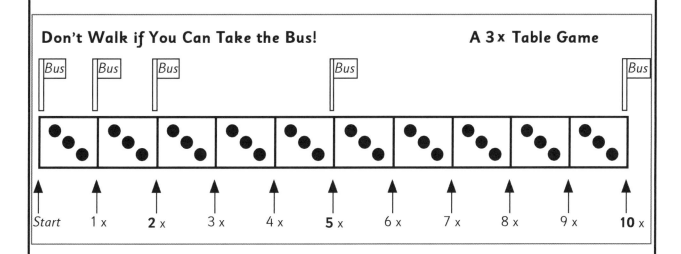

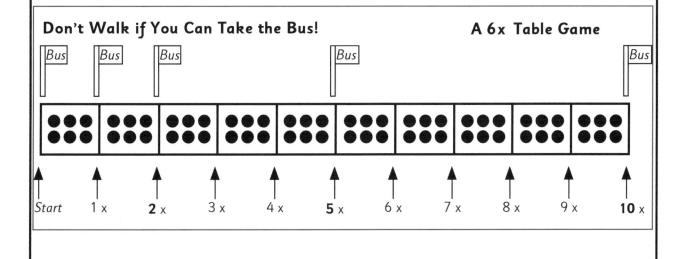

67 MAD Puzzle

Teaching points

▶ Times tables facts up to 6×6.

▶ Finding factors of given multiples.

▶ The connection between multiplication and division and between factors and products.

▶ Logical reasoning.

Note to member of staff or parent

▶ Make sure that the child begins by completing the practice multiplication grid, without any help or any opportunity to copy answers, in preparation for solving the puzzle.

▶ The completed practice grid must be hidden before the child starts to solve the puzzle. Warn the child in advance that it will not be available once it has been completed.

▶ Make sure that no calculation is attempted by counting in ones, on fingers or otherwise.

▶ The child should use only logic. The puzzles in this book have been carefully designed so that the solver need never resort to guesswork or trial and error.

Equipment needed

A pencil and rubber.

67. MAD Puzzle

Name:

Date:

When to hand it in:

Instructions

Write the factors 2 to 6 in the circles so that each digit appears only once in every horizontal row and no number is repeated in any vertical column. The number shown at the top left of a rectangle enclosing two circles is the product of the two circled numbers.

Before you start: Prepare yourself by filling in the facts on this small multiplication grid, which is part of the familiar 10 x 10 multiplication square. (You need not fill in the square numbers, because the puzzle rules do not allow you to repeat a number in any row or column.)

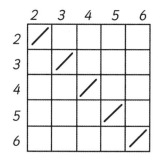

After completing the multiplication grid, fold it back to hide it from view before beginning on the puzzle.

MAD Puzzle   **Digits 2 to 6**

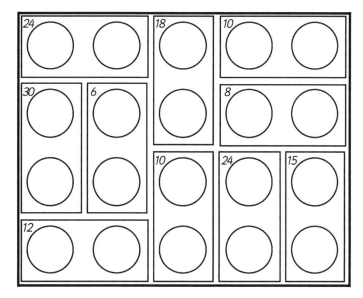

68 The 6x Table Coin Solitaire – a game for 1 player

Teaching points

▶ The 6× table.

▶ Using the step counting model of multiplication tables. Step counting in 6s.

▶ The commutative property of multiplication.

▶ Matching products to multiplication questions, without using the word 'division'.

▶ Practice in deriving the harder tables facts from the known key facts.

Note to member of staff or parent

▶ Make sure the child knows that the key facts of any table are the 2×, 5× and 10× steps (not necessarily in that order) and can confidently tell you the key facts for this table.

▶ During the preparation for the game, i.e. the labelling of the coins, encourage the child to step count (in 6s, not 1s) from 1 × 6. However, while playing the game the child is not allowed to recite the whole table from the beginning, nor to count in ones.

▶ The pre-game practice exercise is to make sure that the child knows how to derive all the necessary facts from the key facts in as few steps of reasoning as possible. For example, to find the answer to 7 × 6 from the nearest key fact, it is quicker to add the two extra groups of 6 as a chunk, leading to the calculation 30 + 12, rather than step count two separate steps forward from 5 × 6.

▶ There is nothing wrong with transposing the questions so that 7 × 6, say, is recognised as being the same as 6 × 7 which can be calculated as 7 more than 35. However, if transposing the digits results in frequent errors, encourage the child to think of all the questions as belonging firmly to the 6× table, rather than the 6th step of all the other tables, as outlined in the 'Practice' section on the next page.

▶ During the game, which is essentially a division exercise, the process outlined in the pre-game practice must be inverted. The first step is to find where a product lies in relation to the key facts before calculating how many steps away it is from the nearest key fact.

▶ On each occasion the game is played, the coins should be labelled afresh by the child.

Equipment needed

10 small coins. Round sticky labels of a size to fit on the coins. Also, a 1–10 die or some other way of generating the numbers from 1 to 10 in a random order, for the pre-game practice.

68. The 6x Table Coin Solitaire

Name:

Date:

Instructions

Practice: Practise deriving all the steps of the 6x table from the key facts, like this:
- 5x is half of 10x
- 2x and 4x (and 8x, if you like) are found by doubling and redoubling
- 9x is one step less than 10x
- 3x and 6x are one step more than a key fact
- 7x and 8x are 2 or 3 steps more than a key fact.

Use a 1–10 die, or a shuffled stack of digit cards showing numbers from 1 to 10, to help you practise finding all the steps of this multiplication table in a random order.

Preparation: Attach stickers to one side of 10 small coins. Write the multiples from the 6x tables (i.e. the answers to the questions on the game board below) on the stickers, one product to each coin. Turn the coins over and mix them.

Rules: Pick up a coin, and place it on top of the matching pair of questions (or on top of the single question if the multiple is a square number). When there are only two coins remaining, slide one under the bottom corner of the page and try to predict what number is on the hidden coin. Play on to find if you guessed right.

You should be able to win roughly half the games you play.

The 6x Table Coin Solitaire

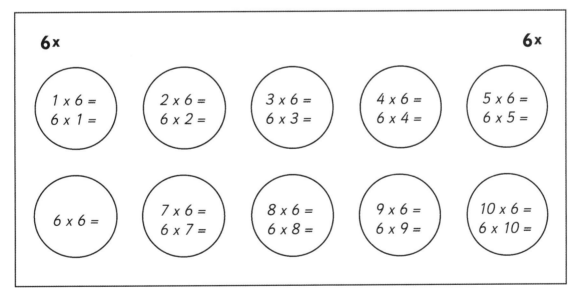

6x   6x

| 1 x 6 =
6 x 1 = | 2 x 6 =
6 x 2 = | 3 x 6 =
6 x 3 = | 4 x 6 =
6 x 4 = | 5 x 6 =
6 x 5 = |

| 6 x 6 = | 7 x 6 =
6 x 7 = | 8 x 6 =
6 x 8 = | 9 x 6 =
6 x 9 = | 10 x 6 =
6 x 10 = |

Hiding place for the final coin

69 MAD Puzzle

Teaching points

❱ Times tables facts up to 6 × 6.

❱ Finding factors of given multiples.

❱ The connection between multiplication and division and between factors and products.

❱ Logical reasoning.

Note to member of staff or parent

❱ Make sure that the child begins by completing the practice multiplication grid, without any help or any opportunity to copy answers, in preparation for solving the puzzle.

❱ The completed practice grid must be hidden before the child starts to solve the puzzle. Warn the child in advance that it will not be available once it has been completed.

❱ Make sure that no calculation is attempted by counting in ones, on fingers or otherwise.

❱ The child should use only logic. The puzzles in this book have been carefully designed so that the solver need never resort to guesswork or trial and error.

Equipment needed

A pencil and rubber.

69. MAD Puzzle

Name:

Date:

When to hand it in:

Instructions

Write the factors 2 to 6 in the circles so that each digit appears only once in each row and each column. The number shown at the top left of a rectangle enclosing two circles is the product of the two circled numbers.

Before you start: Prepare yourself by filling in the facts on this small multiplication grid, which is part of the familiar 10 x 10 multiplication square. (You need not fill in the square numbers, because the puzzle rules do not allow you to repeat a number in any row or column.)

After completing the multiplication grid, fold it back to hide it from view before beginning on the puzzle.

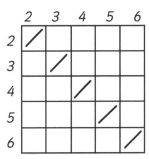

MAD Puzzle

Digits 2 to 6

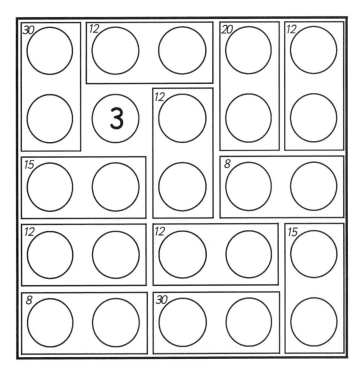

70   The 3 & 6 Times Tables Race – a game for 2 players

Teaching points

▶ The 3× and the 6× tables.

▶ The relationship between the two tables, i.e. that the answer to any step in the 6× table is double the same step of the 3× table.

▶ Practice in deriving difficult tables facts by reasoning from key facts.

Please note that this game is designed for pupils who have already been taught how to reason about multiplication tables through concrete materials and who are now at the stage of using visualisation techniques in order to find answers mentally.

Note to member of staff or parent

▶ Make sure the child knows that the key facts of any table are the 2×, 5× and 10× steps (not necessarily in that order) and can confidently tell you the key facts of both these tables.

▶ Make sure the child knows how to derive answers from the key facts in as few steps as possible.

▶ Do not allow the child to count in ones or to chant a whole table starting from the beginning.

▶ Make sure the child notices the relationship between the two tables as you play the game.

▶ On each turn, players must announce both possible answers aloud, even though only one of the answers can be covered by a counter during the turn.

▶ The game should be played more than twice – once on each board – and on more than one occasion.

Equipment needed

Two ordinary 6-sided dice on which the 6s are each covered with a blank sticker, to represent zero. Counters, preferably semi-transparent, that fit on the squares of the game boards.

70. The 3 & 6 Times Tables Race

Name:

Date:

Instructions

On two dice, cover the 6s with blank stickers. Choose a board. Take turns to throw both dice and throw again if both show a blank. The total of both dice is the number you must now multiply by 3 and by 6. So, if the total amount on both dice is 5, announce that 5 x 3 = 15 and 5 x 6 = 30. Place a counter on either one of these answers. If both products are already covered, you can do nothing on this turn. The winner is the first player to place four counters in a row, horizontally, vertically or diagonally. Swap boards and play again.

The 3 x and 6 x Tables   *Player 1*

27	30	42	6
54	12	18	36
3	21	24	60
15	48	9	30

The 3 x and 6 x Tables   *Player 2*

12	48	18	30
30	15	42	9
6	24	36	27
60	21	3	54

The Dyscalculia Resource Book © Ronit Bird, 2011 (SAGE)

71 MAD Puzzle

Teaching points

▶ Times tables facts up to 6 × 6.

▶ Finding factors of given multiples.

▶ The connection between multiplication and division and between factors and products.

▶ Logical reasoning.

Note to member of staff or parent

▶ Make sure that the child begins by completing the practice multiplication grid, without any help or any opportunity to copy answers, in preparation for solving the puzzle.

▶ The completed practice grid must be hidden before the child starts to solve the puzzle. Warn the child in advance that it will not be available once it has been completed.

▶ Make sure that no calculation is attempted by counting in ones, on fingers or otherwise.

▶ The child should use only logic. The puzzles in this book have been carefully designed so that the solver need never resort to guesswork or trial and error.

Equipment needed

A pencil and rubber.

71. MAD Puzzle

Name:

Date:

When to hand it in:

Instructions

Write the factors 2 to 6 in the circles so that each digit appears only once in each row and each column. The number shown at the top left of a rectangle enclosing two circles is the product of the two circled numbers.

Before you start: Prepare yourself by filling in the facts on this small multiplication grid, which is part of the familiar 10 x 10 multiplication square. (You need not fill in the square numbers, because the puzzle rules do not allow you to repeat a number in any row or column.)

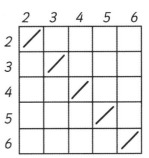

After completing the multiplication grid, fold it back to hide it from view before beginning on the puzzle.

MAD Puzzle   **Digits 2 to 6**

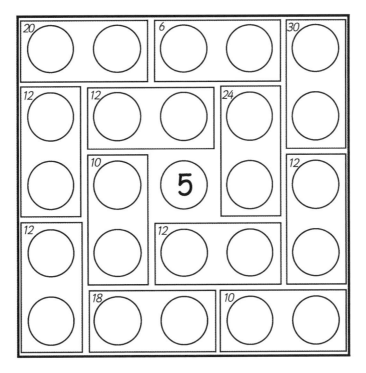

72   Butterfly Doubles [7–9] – a game for 2 players

Teaching points

▶ Doubling the numbers 7, 8 and 9.

▶ Halving the hardest even numbers below 20, i.e. 14, 16 and 18.

▶ The number 7½ lies halfway between 7 and 8, and 8½ lies halfway between 8 and 9.

Note to member of staff or parent

▶ Counting in ones, on fingers or otherwise, is not allowed.

▶ Make sure all the doubles are written inside the butterflies on both boards before any recording of halves is begun.

▶ The child is the one who should write the half numbers on both game boards and work out both players' scores, with as little help as possible.

Equipment needed

A die on which the numbers 7, 8 and 9 each appear twice (either write on stickers that cover the faces of an ordinary die or write on a blank die). A pencil.

72. Butterfly Doubles [7 – 9]

Name:

Date:

When to hand it in:

Instructions

Take turns to throw a die showing only the numbers 7, 8 and 9. Write double the number you throw inside a butterfly shape. After nine turns each, write under every butterfly what the original die throw must have been, i.e. find half of the recorded numbers. Your score is whichever of this second set of numbers occurs most frequently. If two numbers have the same frequency, your score is the number halfway between them, e.g. the same quantity of 8s as 9s means you score 8½. The winner is the player with the higher score.

73   MAD Puzzle

Teaching points

▶ Times tables facts up to 6 × 6.

▶ Finding factors of given multiples.

▶ The connection between multiplication and division and between factors and products.

▶ Logical reasoning.

Note to member of staff or parent

▶ Make sure that the child begins by completing the practice multiplication grid, without any help or any opportunity to copy answers, in preparation for solving the puzzle.

▶ The completed practice grid must be hidden before the child starts to solve the puzzle. Warn the child in advance that it will not be available once it has been completed.

▶ Make sure that no calculation is attempted by counting in ones, on fingers or otherwise.

▶ As the child works through the puzzle, any way of distinguishing between possible answers and final answers is acceptable, but a suggested method is to write the possibilities very lightly and very small and to rub out these digits once a conclusion has been reached.

▶ The child should use only logic. The puzzles in this book have been carefully designed so that the solver need never resort to guesswork or trial and error.

Equipment needed

A pencil and rubber.

73. MAD Puzzle

Name:

Date:

When to hand it in:

Instructions

Write the factors 1 to 6 in the circles so that each digit appears only once in every horizontal row and no number is repeated in any vertical column. The number shown at the top left of a rectangle enclosing two circles is the product of the two circled numbers.

Before you start: Prepare yourself by filling in the facts on this small multiplication grid, which is part of the familiar 10 x 10 multiplication square. (You need not fill in the square numbers, because the puzzle rules do not allow you to repeat a number in any row or column.)

After completing the multiplication grid, fold it back to hide it from view before beginning on the puzzle.

	1	2	3	4	5	6
1	/					
2		/				
3			/			
4				/		
5					/	
6						/

MAD Puzzle   **Digits 1 to 6**

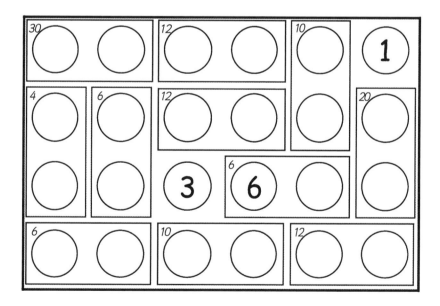

74   Tables on a Number Line – a game for 2 players

Teaching points

▶ The three hardest multiplication tables, i.e. the 6×, 7× and 8× tables.

▶ A step counting model of the multiplication tables, on an empty number line.

▶ Practice in deriving a new tables fact by adding one step onto the previous multiple.

▶ Using the bridging technique, where appropriate, to find the next multiple.

▶ Picking up the step count at different starting points, not at the beginning of the table.

Note to member of staff or parent

▶ Make sure the child understands what each number line on the game board represents. It may help the child prepare for the game if you sketch out a blank number line with ten equal jumps, as shown here, and encourage the child to use it to work through the 6× or the 8× table, labelling the jumps, the multiples and any bridging that is required.

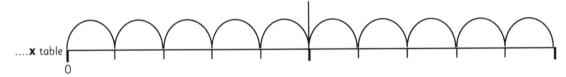

▶ Use the word 'multiple' often during play to describe the numbers in the boxes.

▶ Point out to the child the symmetrical nature of the jumps on either side of the midpoint. The halfway marker is there to help highlight the reflective symmetry of each table.

▶ Note that the number of jumps, determined by the throw of the die, applies to the jumps drawn in black on the game board. The grey arcs are included only to help players navigate along the line and to give the child a sense of a multiplication table modelled as 10 consecutive steps, or jumps, of equal size.

▶ The game board may look daunting, and may benefit from being enlarged when copied, but the game is not difficult to play. It is simply a kind of relay race played by opponents along the three number lines, taken one after the other.

Equipment needed

A 1–3 die, or an ordinary die altered to show each of the digits 1, 2 and 3 twice each (use sticky labels or write on a blank die). Two coloured pens or pencils.

74. Tables on a Number Line

Name:

Date:

When to hand it in:

Instructions

Take turns to throw a 1–3 die. The number on the die is the number of jumps, represented by black arcs (not grey), that you may advance on this turn. Each player uses a different colour of pen or pencil for writing labels on the game board below.

Start at the beginning of the 6x table and label the number of jumps that matches your die throw: label the size of the jumps above each arc, then record under the number line where each jump lands, which sometimes means writing a multiple in one of the boxes. If your turn ends at a place that is not a multiple, you must still label under the number line the number at which the jump (a bridging jump) lands. Each player's move continues from the previous player's move, i.e. from the most recently labelled spot. The player who reaches the end of the 6x or 7x number line will find the final box already completed; when this happens, stop, in the middle of the turn if necessary, and go on to have an extra turn to throw the die. Begin the extra turn on the next number line, making a start on the next multiplication table.

The game ends when one player reaches or passes the end of the 8x table number line. The winner is the player who has written the most multiples, i.e. has completed the most boxes.

Tables on a Number Line

6 x table

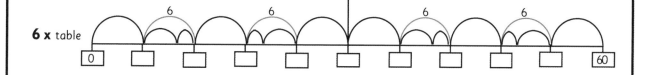

7 x table

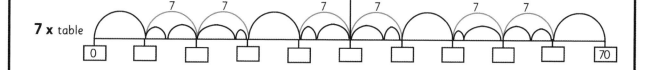

8 x table

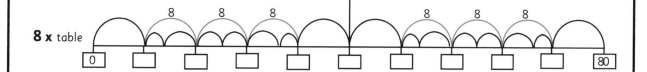

75   MAD Puzzle

Teaching points

▌ Times tables facts up to 6 × 6.

▌ Finding factors of given multiples.

▌ The connection between multiplication and division and between factors and products.

▌ Logical reasoning.

Note to member of staff or parent

▌ Make sure that the child begins by completing the practice multiplication grid, without any help or any opportunity to copy answers, in preparation for solving the puzzle.

▌ The completed practice grid must be hidden before the child starts to solve the puzzle. Warn the child in advance that it will not be available once it has been completed.

▌ Make sure that no calculation is attempted by counting in ones, on fingers or otherwise.

▌ As the child works through the puzzle, any way of distinguishing between possible answers and final answers is acceptable, but a suggested method is to write the possibilities very lightly and very small and to rub out these digits once a conclusion has been reached.

▌ The child should use only logic. The puzzles in this book have been carefully designed so that the solver need never resort to guesswork or trial and error.

Equipment needed

A pencil and rubber.

75. MAD Puzzle

Name:

Date:

When to hand it in:

Instructions

Write the factors 1 to 6 in the circles so that each digit appears only once in every horizontal row and no number is repeated in any vertical column. The number shown at the top left of a rectangle enclosing two circles is the product of the two circled numbers.

Before you start: Prepare yourself by filling in the facts on this small multiplication grid, which is part of the familiar 10 x 10 multiplication square. (You need not fill in the square numbers, because the puzzle rules do not allow you to repeat a number in any row or column.)

After completing the multiplication grid, fold it back to hide it from view before beginning on the puzzle.

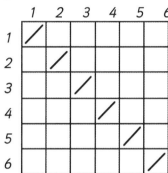

MAD Puzzle   **Digits 1 to 6**

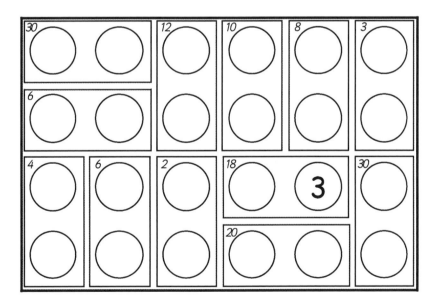

76 The 7x Table Coin Solitaire – a game for 1 player

Teaching points

▶ The 7× table.

▶ Using the step counting model of multiplication tables. Step counting in 7s.

▶ The commutative property of multiplication.

▶ Matching products to multiplication questions, without using the word 'division'.

▶ Practice in deriving the harder tables facts from the known key facts.

Note to member of staff or parent

▶ Make sure the child knows that the key facts of any table are the 2×, 5× and 10× steps (not necessarily in that order) and can confidently tell you the key facts for this table.

▶ During the preparation for the game, i.e. the labelling of the coins, encourage the child to step count (in 7s, not 1s) from 1 × 7. However, while playing the game do not allow the child to recite the whole table from the beginning, nor to count in ones.

▶ The pre-game practice exercise is to make sure that the child knows how to derive all the necessary facts from the key facts in as few steps of reasoning as possible. For example, to find the answer to 7 × 7 from the key fact 5 × 7, it is better to add the two extra groups of 7 as a chunk, leading to the calculation 35 + 14, rather than step count two separate steps forward from 5 × 7 = 35.

▶ During the game, which is essentially a division exercise, the process outlined in the pre-game practice must be inverted. The first step is to find where a product lies in relation to the key facts before calculating how many steps away it is from the nearest key fact.

▶ The game should be played more than once and on more than one occasion. On each occasion the coins should be labelled afresh by the child.

Equipment needed

10 small coins. Round sticky labels of a size to fit on the coins. Also, a 1–10 die or some other way of generating the numbers from 1 to 10 in a random order, for the pre-game practice.

76. The 7x Table Coin Solitaire

Name:

Date:

Instructions

Practice: Practise deriving all the steps of the 7x table from the key facts, like this:
- 5x is half of 10x
- 2x and 4x (and 8x, if you like) are found by doubling and redoubling
- 9x is one step less than 10x
- 3x and 6x are one step more than a key fact
- 7x and 8x are 2 or 3 steps more than a key fact.

Use a 1–10 die, or a shuffled stack of digit cards showing numbers from 1 to 10, to help you practise finding all the steps of this multiplication table in a random order.

Preparation: Attach stickers to one side of 10 small coins. Write the multiples from the 7x tables (i.e. the answers to the questions on the game board below) on the stickers, one product to each coin. Turn the coins over and mix them.

Rules: Pick up a coin, and place it on top of the matching pair of questions (or on top of the single question if the multiple is a square number). When there are only two coins remaining, slide one under the bottom corner of the page and try to predict what number is on the hidden coin. Play on to find if you guessed right.

You should be able to win roughly half the games you play.

The 7x Table Coin Solitaire

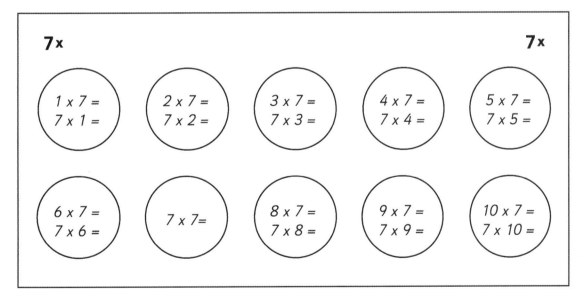

77   MAD Puzzle

Teaching points

▶ Times tables facts up to 7×7.

▶ Finding factors of given multiples.

▶ The connection between multiplication and division and between factors and products.

▶ Logical reasoning.

Note to member of staff or parent

▶ Make sure that the child begins by completing the practice multiplication grid, without any help or any opportunity to copy answers, in preparation for solving the puzzle.

▶ The completed practice grid must be hidden before the child starts to solve the puzzle. Warn the child in advance that it will not be available once it has been completed.

▶ Make sure that no calculation is attempted by counting in ones, on fingers or otherwise.

▶ The child should use only logic. The puzzles in this book have been carefully designed so that the solver need never resort to guesswork or trial and error.

Equipment needed

A pencil and rubber.

77. MAD Puzzle

Name:

Date:

When to hand it in:

Instructions

Write the factors 2 to 7 in the circles so that each digit appears only once in every horizontal row and no number is repeated in any vertical column. The number shown at the top left of a rectangle enclosing two circles is the product of the two circled numbers.

Before you start: Prepare yourself by filling in the facts on this small multiplication grid, which is part of the familiar 10 x 10 multiplication square. (You need not fill in the square numbers, because the puzzle rules do not allow you to repeat a number in any row or column.)

After completing the multiplication grid, fold it back before beginning on the puzzle.

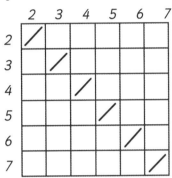

MAD Puzzle

Digits 2 to 7

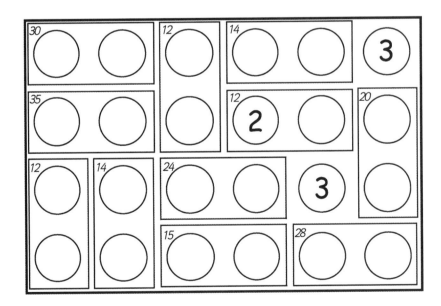

78 Compete for the Harder Facts of the 7x Table – a game for 2 players

Teaching points

▶ The harder facts of the 7x table, i.e. from 6 × 7 to 9 × 7.

▶ Practice in deriving difficult tables facts by reasoning from key facts.

Please note that this game has been designed for pupils who have already been taught how to reason about multiplication tables through concrete materials and who are now ready to use visualisation techniques in order to find answers mentally.

Note to member of staff or parents

▶ Make sure the child is able to tell you the key facts of the 7x table.

▶ Make sure the child knows how to derive answers from the key facts in as few steps as possible. For example, to find the answer to 8 × 7 (arguably the hardest tables fact of them all) add the three extra groups of 7 that lie beyond the key fact of 5 × 7 as a whole chunk, leading to the calculation 35 + 21. This is much more efficient than counting on three separate steps of 7 starting from 35.

▶ If an answer seems to take a suspiciously long time to find, challenge the child to explain how the answer was derived from a key fact. No fact may be recorded on the game board unless it was found without counting in ones and without having to chant the whole table starting from 1 × 7.

▶ The players record each fact in digits, first as multiplication and later as division. A second die throw of 6, say, could result in two outcomes: either both the boxes labelled with a 6 could be started (with both containing identical records of the multiplication fact) or one of the boxes could be completed, in which case it would look like this:

▶ The game boards can be easily copied onto paper so that the game can be played as often as required.

Equipment needed

A die altered to show the following digits (use sticky labels to cover the faces of an ordinary die or write on a blank die): two 7s, two 8s, one 6 and one 9. A pencil.

78. Compete for the Harder Facts of the 7x Table

Name:

Date:

When to hand it in:

Instructions

Alter a die to show a 6, two 7s, two 8s and a 9. Label the eight boxes on your board using the four numbers 6, 7, 8 and 9 twice each, in any order you choose. Take turns to throw the die and multiply the number thrown by 7. In either one of the two boxes labelled the same as your die throw, write the multiplication question and answer in digits. When the same number comes up again, you may write the related division fact in the same box, or the multiplication fact in the alternative box. The winner is the first player with five boxes in a row in which both the multiplication and the division facts are recorded.

Compete for the Harder Facts of the 7x Table

Player 1

Player 2

79   MAD Puzzle

Teaching points

▶ Times tables facts up to 7×7.

▶ Finding factors of given multiples.

▶ The connection between multiplication and division and between factors and products.

▶ Logical reasoning.

Note to member of staff or parent

▶ Make sure that the child begins by completing the practice multiplication grid, without any help or any opportunity to copy answers, in preparation for solving the puzzle.

▶ The completed practice grid must be hidden before the child starts to solve the puzzle. Warn the child in advance that it will not be available once it has been completed.

▶ Make sure that no calculation is attempted by counting in ones, on fingers or otherwise.

▶ The child should use only logic. The puzzles in this book have been carefully designed so that the solver need never resort to guesswork or trial and error.

Equipment needed

A pencil and rubber.

79. MAD Puzzle

Name:

Date:

When to hand it in:

Instructions

Write the factors 2 to 7 in the circles so that each digit appears only once in every horizontal row and no number is repeated in any vertical column. The number shown at the top left of a rectangle enclosing two circles is the product of the two circled numbers.

Before you start: Prepare yourself by filling in the facts on this small multiplication grid, which is part of the familiar 10 x 10 multiplication square. (You need not fill in the square numbers, because the puzzle rules do not allow you to repeat a number in any row or column.)

After completing the multiplication grid, fold it back before beginning on the puzzle.

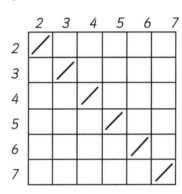

MAD Puzzle   **Digits 2 to 7**

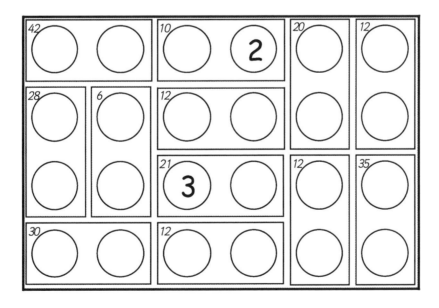

80 Advanced Doubling & Halving Track Race – a game for 2 or 3 players

Teaching points

▶ Mental doubling of numbers in which the units' digit is greater than 5.

▶ Mental halving of numbers in which there are an odd number of tens.

▶ Halving the odd numbers 1, 3 and 5.

▶ Double and half questions mixed together.

Please note that this game has been designed for pupils who have already been taught about partitioning and recombining quantities in connection with doubling and halving and who are familiar with easily visualised methods to support their thinking, such as the informal triad and arrow notations shown in earlier games.

Note to member of staff or parent

▶ Make sure that all the double and half facts up to 10 + 10 are secure.

▶ Encourage the child to tackle the harder numbers in this game by using visualisation to practise the doubling and halving strategies that have already been taught.

▶ Make sure the child understands the strategies that have been taught and is able to explain what they are. Do not ask for an explanation after every turn, but do ask whenever the child offers a guess or an incorrect answer.

▶ Although no guesswork is allowed, it is perfectly acceptable to find new answers by reasoning from previous answers or from known facts, provided that the child can explain the reasoning process.

▶ Make sure the child understands how to halve the odd numbers below 10. For this game, the child needs to know how to find that half of 1 is ½, half of 3 is 1½ and half of 5 is 2½.

▶ The game should be played more than once and on more than one occasion.

Equipment needed

An ordinary 6-sided die. A token for each player.

80. Advanced Doubling & Halving Track Race

Name:

Date:

Instructions

Start with the players' tokens at the top left of the track. Take turns to throw a die and move your token to match the throw. Double or half the number you land on according to the instructions on the board. If your answer is wrong, your token must be replaced where it was at the start of the turn. The winner is the first to travel around the whole track twice.

Before you start you may need to practise the advanced doubling and halving techniques, i.e.
- how to double a number in which the units' digit is greater than 5
- how to find half of a number in which one or more of the digits is an odd number.

Advanced Doubling & Halving Track Race

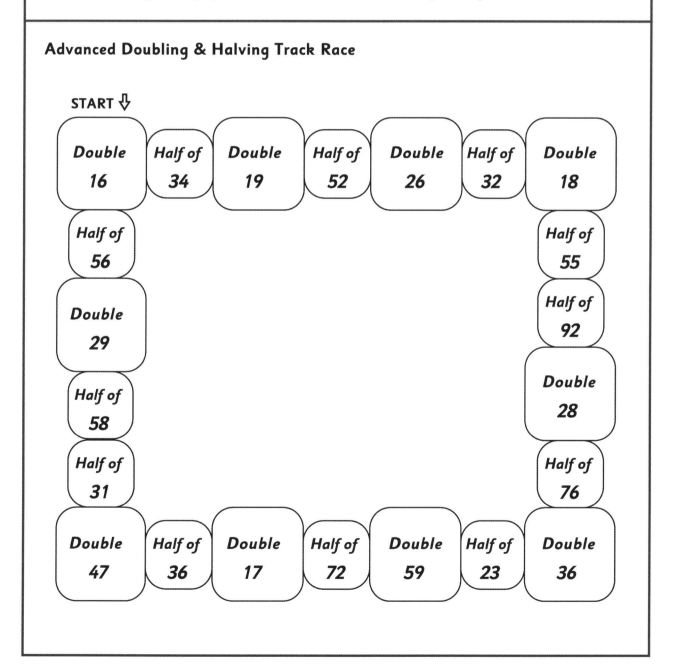

START ⇩

Double 16	Half of 34	Double 19	Half of 52	Double 26	Half of 32	Double 18

Half of 56 — Double 29 — Half of 58 — Half of 31

Half of 55 — Half of 92 — Double 28 — Half of 76

| Double 47 | Half of 36 | Double 17 | Half of 72 | Double 59 | Half of 23 | Double 36 |

81   MAD Puzzle

Teaching points

▶ Times tables facts up to 7×7.

▶ Finding factors of given multiples.

▶ The connection between multiplication and division and between factors and products.

▶ Logical reasoning.

Note to member of staff or parent

▶ Make sure that the child begins by completing the practice multiplication grid, without any help or any opportunity to copy answers, in preparation for solving the puzzle.

▶ The completed practice grid must be hidden before the child starts to solve the puzzle. Warn the child in advance that it will not be available once it has been completed.

▶ Make sure that no calculation is attempted by counting in ones, on fingers or otherwise.

▶ The child should use only logic. The puzzles in this book have been carefully designed so that the solver need never resort to guesswork or trial and error.

Equipment needed

A pencil and rubber.

81. MAD Puzzle

Name:

Date:

When to hand it in:

Instructions

Write the factors 2 to 7 in the circles so that each digit appears only once in every horizontal row and no number is repeated in any vertical column. The number shown at the top left of a rectangle enclosing two circles is the product of the two circled numbers.

Before you start: Prepare yourself by filling in the facts on this small multiplication grid, which is part of the familiar 10 x 10 multiplication square. (You need not fill in the square numbers, because the puzzle rules do not allow you to repeat a number in any row or column.)

After completing the multiplication grid, fold it back before beginning on the puzzle.

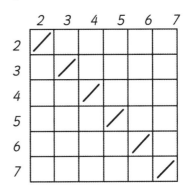

MAD Puzzle

Digits 2 to 7

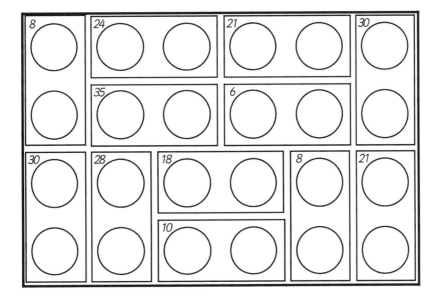

82 The 8x Table Coin Solitaire – a game for 1 player

Teaching points

▶ The 8× table.

▶ Using the step counting model of multiplication tables. Step counting in 8s.

▶ The commutative property of multiplication.

▶ Matching products to multiplication questions, without using the word 'division'.

▶ Practice in deriving the harder tables facts from the known key facts.

Note to member of staff or parent

▶ Make sure the child knows that the key facts of any table are the 2×, 5× and 10× steps (not necessarily in that order) and can confidently tell you the key facts for this table.

▶ During the preparation for the game, i.e. the labelling of the coins, encourage the child to step count (in 8s, not 1s) from 1 × 8. However, while playing the game do not allow the child to recite the whole table from the beginning, nor to count in ones.

▶ The pre-game practice exercise is to make sure that the child knows how to derive all the necessary facts in as few steps of reasoning as possible. For example, 8 times any number can be found by finding double 4 times the same number, which in turn is found by doubling 2 times the same number. Alternatively, the child can work from a key fact in just the same way as for any other times table, so, for example, to find 7 × 8 (arguably the hardest tables fact of them all) simply add two extra 8s, as a chunk, to 5 × 8, leading to the calculation 40 + 16.

▶ During the game, which is essentially a division exercise, the process outlined in the pre-game practice must be inverted. The first step is to find where a product lies in relation to the key facts before calculating how many steps away it is from the nearest key fact.

▶ The game should be played more than once and on more than one occasion. On each occasion the coins should be labelled afresh by the child.

Equipment needed

10 small coins. Round sticky labels of a size to fit on the coins. Also, a 1–10 die or some other way of generating the numbers from 1 to 10 in a random order, for the pre-game practice.

82. The 8x Table Coin Solitaire

Name:

Date:

Instructions

Practice: Practise deriving all the steps of the 8x table from the key facts, like this:
- 5x is half of 10x
- 2x and 4x (and 8x, if you like) are found by doubling and redoubling
- 9x is one step less than 10x
- 3x and 6x are one step more than a key fact
- 7x and 8x are 2 or 3 steps more than a key fact.

Use a 1–10 die, or a shuffled stack of digit cards showing numbers from 1 to 10, to help you practise finding all the steps of this multiplication table in a random order.

Preparation: Attach stickers to one side of 10 small coins. Write the multiples from the 8x tables (i.e. the answers to the questions on the game board below) on the stickers, one product to each coin. Turn the coins over and mix them.

Rules: Pick up a coin, and place it on top of the matching pair of questions (or on top of the single question if the multiple is a square number). When there are only two coins remaining, slide one under the bottom corner of the page and try to predict what number is on the hidden coin. Play on to find if you guessed right.

You should be able to win roughly half the games you play.

The 8x Table Coin Solitaire

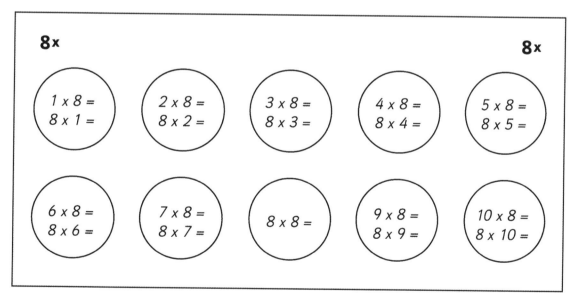

83   MAD Puzzle

Teaching points

◗ Times tables facts up to 7×7.

◗ Finding factors of given multiples.

◗ The connection between multiplication and division and between factors and products.

◗ Logical reasoning.

Note to member of staff or parent

◗ Make sure that the child begins by completing the practice multiplication grid, without any help or any opportunity to copy answers, in preparation for solving the puzzle.

◗ The completed practice grid must be hidden before the child starts to solve the puzzle. Warn the child in advance that it will not be available once it has been completed.

◗ Make sure that no calculation is attempted by counting in ones, on fingers or otherwise.

◗ The child should use only logic. The puzzles in this book have been carefully designed so that the solver need never resort to guesswork or trial and error.

Equipment needed

A pencil and rubber.

83. MAD Puzzle

Name:

Date:

When to hand it in:

Instructions
Write the factors 2 to 7 in the circles so that each digit appears only once in every horizontal row and no number is repeated in any vertical column. The number shown at the top left of a rectangle enclosing two circles is the product of the two circled numbers.

Before you start: Prepare yourself by filling in the facts on this small multiplication grid, which is part of the familiar 10 x 10 multiplication square. (You need not fill in the square numbers, because the puzzle rules do not allow you to repeat a number in any row or column.)

After completing the multiplication grid, fold it back before beginning on the puzzle.

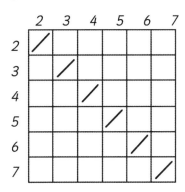

MAD Puzzle   **Digits 2 to 7**

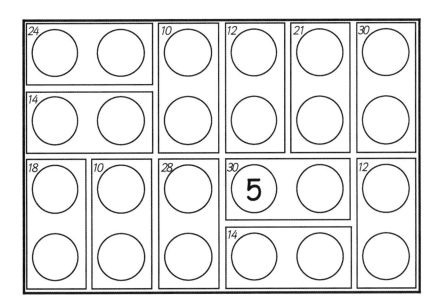

84   Compete for the Harder Facts of the 8x Table – a game for 2 players

Teaching points

▎ The harder facts of the 8× table, i.e. from 6 × 8 to 9 × 8.

▎ Practice in deriving difficult tables facts by reasoning from key facts.

Note to member of staff or parents

▎ Make sure the child is able to tell you the key facts of the 8× table.

▎ Make sure the child knows how to derive answers from the key facts in as few steps as possible. For example, to find the answer to 7 × 8 (arguably the hardest tables fact of them all) add the two extra groups of 8 that lie beyond the key fact of 5 × 8 as a whole chunk, leading to the easy calculation 40 + 16.

▎ If an answer seems to take a suspiciously long time to find, challenge the child to explain how the answer was derived from a key fact. No fact may be recorded on the game board unless it was found without counting in ones and without having to chant the whole table starting from 1 × 8.

▎ The players record each fact in digits, first as multiplication and later as division. A second die throw of 6, say, could result in two outcomes: either both the boxes labelled with a 6 could be started (with both containing identical records of the multiplication fact) or one of the boxes could be completed, in which case it would look like this:

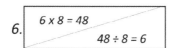

6.   6 x 8 = 48

           48 ÷ 8 = 6

▎ The game boards can be easily copied onto paper so that the game can be played as often as required.

Equipment needed

A die altered to show the following digits (use sticky labels to cover the faces of an ordinary die or write on a blank die): two 7s, two 8s, one 6 and one 9. A pencil.

84. Compete for the Harder Facts of the 8x Table

Name:

Date:

When to hand it in:

Instructions

Alter a die to show a 6, two 7s, two 8s and a 9. Label the eight boxes on your board using the four numbers 6, 7, 8 and 9 twice each, in any order you choose. Take turns to throw the die and multiply the number thrown by 8. In either one of the two boxes labelled the same as your die throw, write the multiplication question and answer in digits. When the same number comes up again, you may write the related division fact in the same box or the multiplication fact in the alternative box. The winner is the first player with five boxes in a row in which both the multiplication and the division facts are recorded.

Compete for the Harder Facts of the 8x Table

Player 1

Player 2

85 MAD Puzzle

Teaching points

▶ Times tables facts up to 7×7.

▶ Finding factors of given multiples.

▶ The connection between multiplication and division and between factors and products.

▶ Logical reasoning.

Note to member of staff or parent

▶ Make sure that the child begins by completing the practice multiplication grid, without any help or any opportunity to copy answers, in preparation for solving the puzzle.

▶ The completed practice grid must be hidden before the child starts to solve the puzzle. Warn the child in advance that it will not be available once it has been completed.

▶ Make sure that no calculation is attempted by counting in ones, on fingers or otherwise.

▶ The child should use only logic. The puzzles in this book have been carefully designed so that the solver need never resort to guesswork or trial and error.

Equipment needed

A pencil and rubber.

85. MAD Puzzle

Name:

Date:

When to hand it in:

Instructions

Write the factors 2 to 7 in the circles so that each digit appears only once in every horizontal row and no number is repeated in any vertical column. The number shown at the top left of a rectangle enclosing two circles is the product of the two circled numbers.

Before you start: Prepare yourself by filling in the facts on this small multiplication grid, which is part of the familiar 10 x 10 multiplication square. (You need not fill in the square numbers, because the puzzle rules do not allow you to repeat a number in any row or column.)

After completing the multiplication grid, fold it back before beginning on the puzzle.

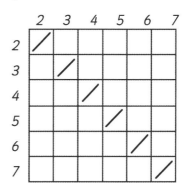

MAD Puzzle   **Digits 2 to 7**

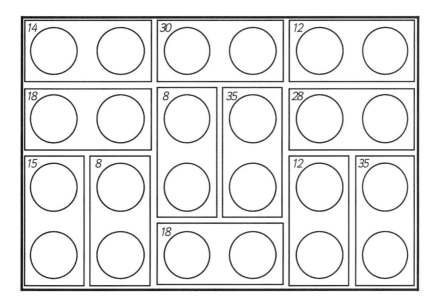

---

86 The 4 & 8 Times Tables Race – a game for 2 players

Teaching points

▶ The 4× and the 8× tables.

▶ The relationship between the two tables, i.e. that the answer to any step in the 8× table is double the same step of the 4× table.

▶ Practice in deriving difficult tables facts by reasoning from key facts.

Note to member of staff or parent

▶ Make sure the child knows the key facts (the 2×, 5× and 10× steps) of both these tables.

▶ Make sure the child knows how to derive answers from the key facts in as few steps as possible.

▶ No counting in ones is allowed, nor is chanting the whole table starting from the beginning.

▶ Make sure the child notices the relationship between the two tables as you play the game.

▶ On each turn, players must announce both possible answers aloud, even though only one of the answers can be covered by a counter during the turn.

▶ The game should be played more than twice – once on each board – and on more than one occasion.

Equipment needed

Two ordinary dice on which the 6s are each covered with a blank sticker, to represent zero. Counters, preferably semi-transparent, that fit on the squares of the game boards.

86. The 4 & 8 Times Tables Race

Name:

Date:

Instructions

On two dice, cover the 6s with blank stickers. Choose a board. Take turns to throw both dice and throw again if both show a blank. The total of both dice is the number you must now multiply by 4 and by 8. So, if the total amount on both dice is 3, announce that 3 x 4 = 12 and 3 x 8 = 24. Place a counter on either one of these answers. If both products are already covered, you can do nothing on this turn. The winner is the first player to place four counters in a row, horizontally, vertically or diagonally. Swap boards and play again.

The 4x and 8x Tables *Player 1*

12	56	28	40
32	20	36	4
40	72	8	24
64	16	48	80

The 4x and 8x Tables *Player 2*

16	40	8	64
28	72	56	20
48	12	80	32
36	4	24	40

87 MAD Puzzle

Teaching points

▶ Times tables facts up to 8 × 8.

▶ Finding factors of given multiples.

▶ The connection between multiplication and division and between factors and products.

▶ Logical reasoning.

Note to member of staff or parent

▶ Make sure that the child begins by completing the practice multiplication grid, without any help or any opportunity to copy answers, in preparation for solving the puzzle.

▶ The completed practice grid must be hidden before the child starts to solve the puzzle. Warn the child in advance that it will not be available once it has been completed.

▶ Make sure that no calculation is attempted by counting in ones, on fingers or otherwise.

▶ The child should use only logic. The puzzles in this book have been carefully designed so that the solver need never resort to guesswork or trial and error.

Equipment needed

A pencil and rubber.

87. MAD Puzzle

Name:

Date:

When to hand it in:

Instructions

Write the factors 3 to 8 in the circles so that each digit appears only once in every horizontal row and no number is repeated in any vertical column. The number shown at the top left of a rectangle enclosing two circles is the product of the two circled numbers.

Before you start: Prepare yourself by filling in the facts on this small multiplication grid, which is part of the familiar 10 x 10 multiplication square. (You need not fill in the square numbers, because the puzzle rules do not allow you to repeat a number in any row or column.)

After completing the multiplication grid, fold it back before beginning on the puzzle.

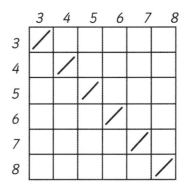

MAD Puzzle   **Digits 3 to 8**

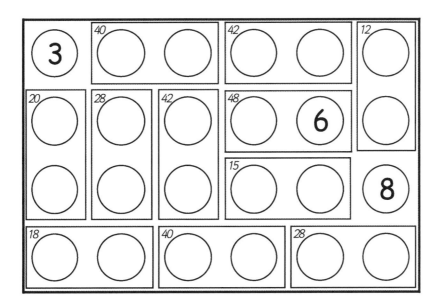

88 Top of the Tables Square – a game for 2 players

Teaching points

▶ The harder facts of the harder multiplication tables, i.e. from 6×6 to 9×9.

▶ The meaning of the terms 'product' and 'multiple'.

▶ Practice in deriving difficult tables facts by reasoning from key facts.

Note to member of staff or parent

▶ Make sure the child is able to tell you the key facts of the 6×, 7×, 8× and 9× tables.

▶ Make sure the child knows how to derive answers from the key facts in as few steps as possible.

▶ When playing the game, use the terms 'product' and 'multiple' often to describe the answers that both players calculate and record on the grid.

▶ If an answer seems to take a suspiciously long time to find, challenge the child to explain how the answer was derived from a key fact. An answer is not allowed to be recorded on the grid unless it was found without resorting to counting in ones and without having to chant a whole table starting from the beginning.

▶ The game boards can be easily copied onto paper so that the game can be played as often as required.

Equipment needed

Two ordinary dice each of which is altered to show the following digits (use sticky labels or write on blank dice): two 7s, two 8s, one 6 and one 9.

88. Top of the Tables Square

Name:

Date:

When to hand it in:

Instructions

Alter two dice to show the following digits: a 6, two 7s, two 8s and a 9 on each die. Take turns to throw the dice and multiply the numbers together. Write the product where the two numbers intersect on your game board. Unless the two numbers on the dice are identical, you will have a choice of two places in which to write the product. Once these spaces are full, you can do nothing on any turn in which the same pair of numbers are thrown. The winner is the first player to write four products in a row, horizontally, vertically or diagonally.

Top of the Tables Square _Player 1_

	6	7	8	9
6				
7				
8				
9				

Top of the Tables Square _Player 2_

	6	7	8	9
6				
7				
8				
9				

89 MAD Puzzle

Teaching points

▶ Times tables facts up to 8×8.

▶ Finding factors of given multiples.

▶ The connection between multiplication and division and between factors and products.

▶ Logical reasoning.

Note to member of staff or parent

▶ Make sure that the child begins by completing the practice multiplication grid, without any help or any opportunity to copy answers, in preparation for solving the puzzle.

▶ The completed practice grid must be hidden before the child starts to solve the puzzle. Warn the child in advance that it will not be available once it has been completed.

▶ Make sure that no calculation is attempted by counting in ones, on fingers or otherwise.

▶ The child should use only logic. The puzzles in this book have been carefully designed so that the solver need never resort to guesswork or trial and error.

Equipment needed

A pencil and rubber.

89. MAD Puzzle

Name:

Date:

When to hand it in:

Instructions

Write the factors 3 to 8 in the circles so that each digit appears only once in every horizontal row and no number is repeated in any vertical column. The number shown at the top left of a rectangle enclosing two circles is the product of the two circled numbers.

Before you start: Prepare yourself by filling in the facts on this small multiplication grid, which is part of the familiar 10 x 10 multiplication square. (You need not fill in the square numbers, because the puzzle rules do not allow you to repeat a number in any row or column.)

After completing the multiplication grid, fold it back before beginning on the puzzle.

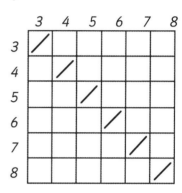

MAD Puzzle   **Digits 3 to 8**

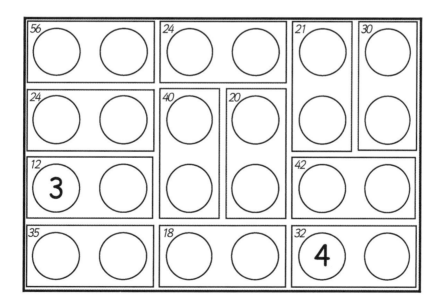

90   Areas on a Grid – a game for 2 or 3 players

Teaching points

▶ The area model of multiplication and division.

▶ Some multiples, such as 12 and 24, appear in more than one multiplication table.

Please note that children should not be asked to play this game unless they have had previous experience of making and reading rectangular arrays, including playing a concrete version of this game with Cuisenaire rods on 1 cm squared paper.

Note to member of staff or parent

▶ There must be no counting in ones, on fingers or otherwise.

▶ Reciting a times table from the beginning can be allowed the first time the child plays this game, but should be discouraged as soon as possible after that.

▶ Note that each number thrown must be represented by a single complete rectangle in this game, e.g. a throw of 6 can only be shaded on the board as one rectangle measuring 1 by 6 squares or 2 by 3 squares, but not as one group of 4 squares alongside another group of 2 squares.

▶ The game boards can be easily copied onto squared paper so that the game can be played as often as required.

▶ Players should take turns to start the game.

▶ The game in which two players share a board is for only 2 players. The variation, in which each player shades an individual board measuring 10 by 10 squares, can be played by more than 2 players.

▶ Once the game and its variation have been played several times, try substituting different multiples for the two smaller numbers on the die, e.g. 15 and 21, or 14 and 20.

Equipment needed

A die on which the following six numbers appear (either write on stickers that cover the faces of an ordinary die or write on a blank die): 6, 8, 12, 16, 18 and 24. Two coloured pencils.

90. Areas on a Grid

Name:

Date:

When to hand it in:

Instructions

Take turns to throw a die on which the following numbers appear: 6, 8, 12, 16, 18 and 24. On the game board, sketch out a single rectangle to match the number thrown and shade it in lightly with your coloured pencil, writing the total area in the middle of the rectangle. So, if you throw a 6 you can colour in an area of six squares as a rectangle measuring either 1 by 6 or 2 by 3, writing 6 at the centre of your shaded area. As soon as one player can no longer find space on the game board to sketch the next rectangle, the other player wins the game.

Variation: Players have individual boards measuring 10 by 10 squares on which to shade rectangular areas to match their die throw. The player who runs out of space first is the loser.

Areas on a Grid

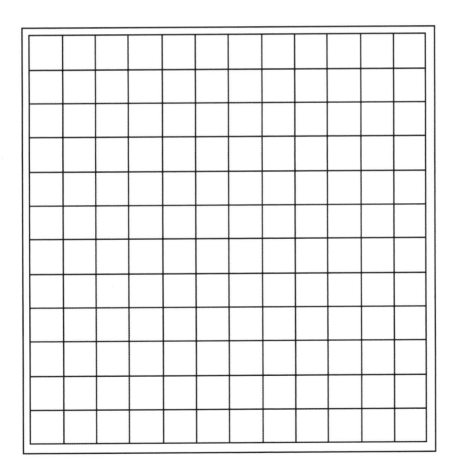

91   MAD Puzzle

Teaching points

▶ Times tables facts up to 8 × 8.

▶ Finding factors of given multiples.

▶ The connection between multiplication and division and between factors and products.

▶ Logical reasoning.

Note to member of staff or parent

▶ Make sure that the child begins by completing the practice multiplication grid, without any help or any opportunity to copy answers, in preparation for solving the puzzle.

▶ The completed practice grid must be hidden before the child starts to solve the puzzle. Warn the child in advance that it will not be available once it has been completed.

▶ Make sure that no calculation is attempted by counting in ones, on fingers or otherwise.

▶ The child should use only logic. The puzzles in this book have been carefully designed so that the solver need never resort to guesswork or trial and error.

Equipment needed

A pencil and rubber.

91. MAD Puzzle

Name:

Date:

When to hand it in:

Instructions

Write the factors 3 to 8 in the circles so that each digit appears only once in every horizontal row and no number is repeated in any vertical column. The number shown at the top left of a rectangle enclosing two circles is the product of the two circled numbers.

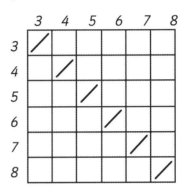

Before you start: Prepare yourself by filling in the facts on this small multiplication grid, which is part of the familiar 10 x 10 multiplication square. (You need not fill in the square numbers, because the puzzle rules do not allow you to repeat a number in any row or column.)

After completing the multiplication grid, fold it back before beginning on the puzzle.

MAD Puzzle   **Digits 3 to 8**

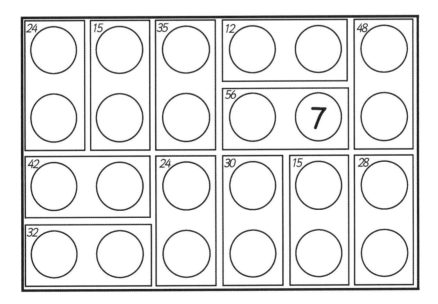

92 MAD Puzzle

Teaching points

▶ Times tables facts up to 8 × 8.

▶ Finding factors of given multiples.

▶ The connection between multiplication and division and between factors and products.

▶ Logical reasoning.

Note to member of staff or parent

▶ Make sure that the child begins by completing the practice multiplication grid, without any help or any opportunity to copy answers, in preparation for solving the puzzle.

▶ The completed practice grid must be hidden before the child starts to solve the puzzle. Warn the child in advance that it will not be available once it has been completed.

▶ Make sure that no calculation is attempted by counting in ones, on fingers or otherwise.

▶ As the child works through the puzzle, any way of distinguishing between possible answers and final answers is acceptable, but a suggested method is to write the possibilities very lightly and very small and to rub out these digits once a conclusion has been reached about any circle.

▶ The child should use only logic. The puzzles in this book have been carefully designed so that the solver need never resort to guesswork or trial and error.

Equipment needed

A pencil and rubber.

92. MAD Puzzle

Name:

Date:

When to hand it in:

Instructions

Write the factors 4 to 8 in the circles so that each digit appears only once in each row and each column. The number shown at the top left of a rectangle enclosing two circles is the product of the two circled numbers.

Before you start: Prepare yourself by filling in the facts on this small multiplication grid, which is part of the familiar 10 x 10 multiplication square. (You need not fill in the square numbers, because the puzzle rules do not allow you to repeat a number in any row or column.)

After completing the multiplication grid, fold it back before beginning on the puzzle.

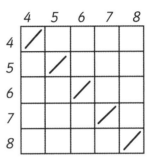

MAD Puzzle

Digits 4 to 8

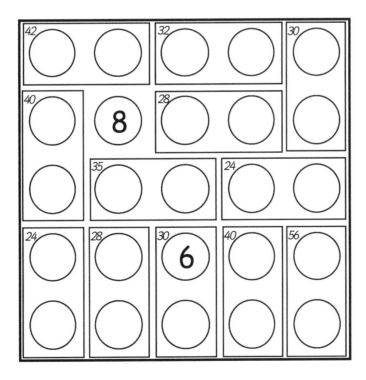

93   Factors Track Race – a game for 2 players

Teaching points

▶ The mathematical meaning of the term 'factor'.

▶ Finding all the factors of a selection of numbers below 40.

▶ Factors for any number always include 1 and the number itself.

▶ Larger numbers do not necessarily have more factors than smaller numbers.

▶ The first five prime numbers.

Note to member of staff or parent

▶ Make sure the child understands the word 'factor' to mean a number that divides exactly into another, leaving no remainder.

▶ The game is designed to be played between an adult and a learner, not between two learners. The child must have the first turn.

▶ Let the child discover for him/herself that factors come in pairs. For example, if the child recognises that 16 must have a factor of 2 because it is an even number, and stops at that, do not point out that 2 must be multiplied by another number to produce 16 and that there-fore 8 is also a factor of 16. However, do model the fact that you are looking for pairs of factors when it is your turn.

▶ Make sure the child notices which numbers on the board have no factors other than 1 and itself (i.e. 2, 3, 5, 7, 11). Use the term 'prime numbers' to describe these numbers and encourage the child to use the term every time either player lands on one of these numbers.

▶ Factors can only be counted once in this game, so a player landing on the square number 4 can only move one space even if 2 is correctly identified as a factor and the player realises that 2 must be multiplied by itself to produce 4. The same applies to the numbers 9 and 25 on the game board.

▶ The game should be played at least twice, with the child having the opportunity to begin on both starting positions on different occasions.

Equipment needed

A coin to toss. Scrap paper and pencil. Two tokens.

93. Factors Track Race

Name:

Date:

Instructions

Begin by tossing a coin. If you toss heads, start on 10 while your opponent starts on 15; if it's tails do the opposite. Take turns to jot down on scrap paper the factors of the number on which your token stands, excluding the factors 1 and the number itself. For every factor that you and your opponent agree upon, move your token forward one space. So, if you find two correct factors, a move of two spaces forwards will complete your turn. However, if you cannot find any factors other than 1 and the number itself, you may move your token one space forward. The winner is the first to reach or pass the end of the track.

Factors Track Race

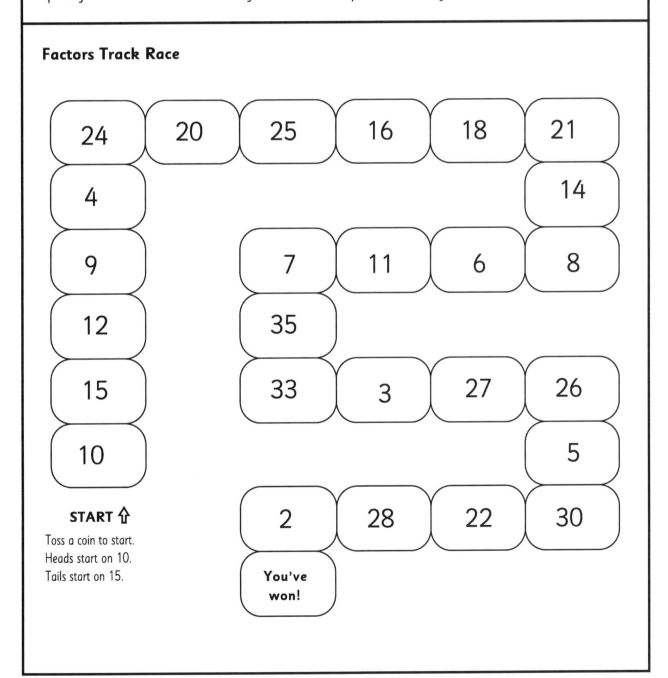

START ⇧

Toss a coin to start.
Heads start on 10.
Tails start on 15.

94   MAD Puzzle

Teaching points

▶ Times tables facts up to 8 × 8.

▶ Finding factors of given multiples.

▶ The connection between multiplication and division and between factors and products.

▶ Logical reasoning.

Note to member of staff or parent

▶ Make sure that the child begins by completing the practice multiplication grid, without any help or any opportunity to copy answers, in preparation for solving the puzzle.

▶ The completed practice grid must be hidden before the child starts to solve the puzzle. Warn the child in advance that it will not be available once it has been completed.

▶ Make sure that no calculation is attempted by counting in ones, on fingers or otherwise.

▶ As the child works through the puzzle, any way of distinguishing between possible answers and final answers is acceptable, but a suggested method is to write the possibilities very lightly and very small and to rub out these digits once a conclusion has been reached about any circle.

▶ The child should use only logic. The puzzles in this book have been carefully designed so that the solver need never resort to guesswork or trial and error.

Equipment needed

A pencil and rubber.

94. MAD Puzzle

Name:

Date:

When to hand it in:

Instructions

Write the factors 4 to 8 in the circles so that each digit appears only once in each row and each column. The number shown at the top left of a rectangle enclosing two circles is the product of the two circled numbers.

Before you start: Prepare yourself by filling in the facts on this small multiplication grid, which is part of the familiar 10 x 10 multiplication square. (You need not fill in the square numbers, because the puzzle rules do not allow you to repeat a number in any row or column.)

After completing the multiplication grid, fold it back before beginning on the puzzle.

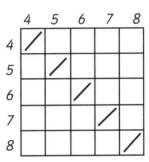

MAD Puzzle   **Digits 4 to 8**

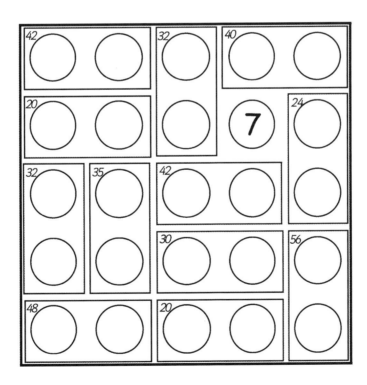

95   MAD Puzzle

Teaching points

- Times tables facts up to 8 × 8.

- Finding factors of given multiples.

- The connection between multiplication and division and between factors and products.

- Logical reasoning.

Note to member of staff or parent

- Make sure that the child begins by completing the practice multiplication grid, without any help or any opportunity to copy answers, in preparation for solving the puzzle.

- The completed practice grid must be hidden before the child starts to solve the puzzle. Warn the child in advance that it will not be available once it has been completed.

- Make sure that no calculation is attempted by counting in ones, on fingers or otherwise.

- As the child works through the puzzle, any way of distinguishing between possible answers and final answers is acceptable, but a suggested method is to write the possibilities very lightly and very small and to rub out these digits once a conclusion has been reached about any circle.

- The child should use only logic. The puzzles in this book have been carefully designed so that the solver need never resort to guesswork or trial and error.

Equipment needed

A pencil and rubber.

95. MAD Puzzle

Name:

Date:

When to hand it in:

Instructions

Write the factors 4 to 8 in the circles so that each digit appears only once in each row and each column. The number shown at the top left of a rectangle enclosing two circles is the product of the two circled numbers.

Before you start: Prepare yourself by filling in the facts on this small multiplication grid, which is part of the familiar 10 x 10 multiplication square. (You need not fill in the square numbers, because the puzzle rules do not allow you to repeat a number in any row or column.)

After completing the multiplication grid, fold it back before beginning on the puzzle.

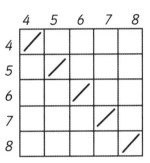

MAD Puzzle   **Digits 4 to 8**

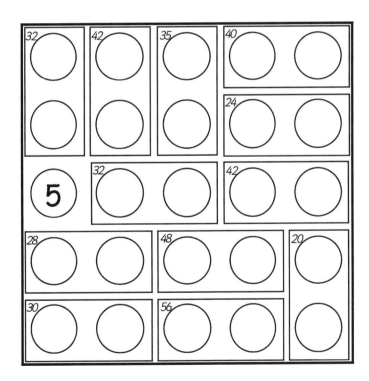

96 MAD Puzzle

Teaching points

▶ Times tables facts up to 8×8.

▶ Finding factors of given multiples.

▶ The connection between multiplication and division and between factors and products.

▶ Logical reasoning.

Note to member of staff or parent

▶ Make sure that the child begins by completing the practice multiplication grid, without any help or any opportunity to copy answers, in preparation for solving the puzzle.

▶ The completed practice grid must be hidden before the child starts to solve the puzzle. Warn the child in advance that it will not be available once it has been completed.

▶ Make sure that no calculation is attempted by counting in ones, on fingers or otherwise.

▶ As the child works through the puzzle, any way of distinguishing between possible answers and final answers is acceptable, but a suggested method is to write the possibilities very lightly and very small and to rub out these digits once a conclusion has been reached about any circle.

▶ The child should use only logic. The puzzles in this book have been carefully designed so that the solver need never resort to guesswork or trial and error.

Equipment needed

A pencil and rubber.

96. MAD Puzzle

Name:

Date:

When to hand it in:

Instructions

Write the factors 4 to 8 in the circles so that each digit appears only once in each row and each column. The number shown at the top left of a rectangle enclosing two circles is the product of the two circled numbers.

Before you start: Prepare yourself by filling in the facts on this small multiplication grid, which is part of the familiar 10 x 10 multiplication square. (You need not fill in the square numbers, because the puzzle rules do not allow you to repeat a number in any row or column.)

After completing the multiplication grid, fold it back before beginning on the puzzle.

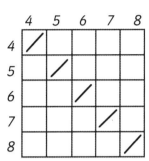

MAD Puzzle **Digits 4 to 8**

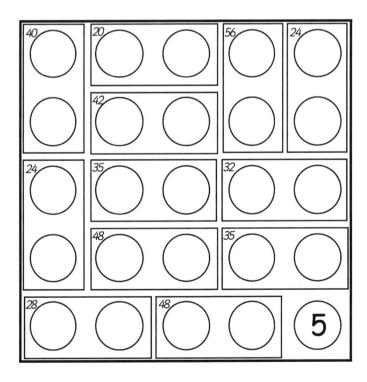

97   MAD Puzzle

Teaching points

▶ Times tables facts up to 8 × 8.

▶ Finding factors of given multiples.

▶ The connection between multiplication and division and between factors and products.

▶ Logical reasoning.

Note to member of staff or parent

▶ Make sure that the child begins by completing the practice multiplication grid, without any help or any opportunity to copy answers, in preparation for solving the puzzle.

▶ The completed practice grid must be hidden before the child starts to solve the puzzle. Warn the child in advance that it will not be available once it has been completed.

▶ Make sure that no calculation is attempted by counting in ones, on fingers or otherwise.

▶ As the child works through the puzzle, any way of distinguishing between possible answers and final answers is acceptable, but a suggested method is to write the possibilities very lightly and very small and to rub out these digits once a conclusion has been reached about any circle.

▶ The child should use only logic. The puzzles in this book have been carefully designed so that the solver need never resort to guesswork or trial and error.

Equipment needed

A pencil and rubber.

97. MAD Puzzle

Name:

Date:

When to hand it in:

Instructions

Write the factors 4 to 8 in the circles so that each digit appears only once in each row and each column. The number shown at the top left of a rectangle enclosing two circles is the product of the two circled numbers.

Before you start: Prepare yourself by filling in the facts on this small multiplication grid, which is part of the familiar 10 x 10 multiplication square. (You need not fill in the square numbers, because the puzzle rules do not allow you to repeat a number in any row or column.)

After completing the multiplication grid, fold it back before beginning on the puzzle.

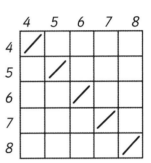

MAD Puzzle   **Digits 4 to 8**

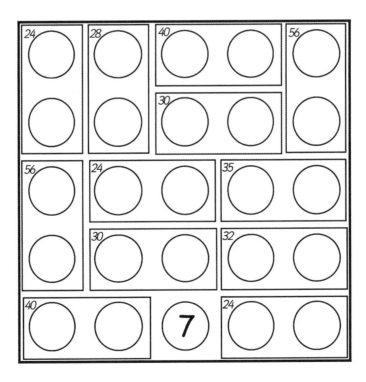

98   MAD Puzzle

Teaching points

▶ Times tables facts up to 9×9.

▶ Finding factors of given multiples.

▶ The connection between multiplication and division and between factors and products.

▶ Logical reasoning.

Note to member of staff or parent

▶ Make sure that the child begins by completing the practice multiplication grid, without any help or any opportunity to copy answers, in preparation for solving the puzzle.

▶ The completed practice grid must be hidden before the child starts to solve the puzzle. Warn the child in advance that it will not be available once it has been completed.

▶ Make sure that no calculation is attempted by counting in ones, on fingers or otherwise.

▶ As the child works through the puzzle, any way of distinguishing between possible answers and final answers is acceptable, but a suggested method is to write the possibilities very lightly and very small and to rub out these digits once a conclusion has been reached about any circle.

▶ The child should use only logic. The puzzles in this book have been carefully designed so that the solver need never resort to guesswork or trial and error.

Equipment needed

A pencil and rubber.

98. MAD Puzzle

Name:

Date:

When to hand it in:

Instructions

Write the factors 5 to 9 in the circles so that each digit appears only once in each row and each column. The number shown at the top left of a rectangle enclosing two circles is the product of the two circled numbers.

Before you start: Prepare yourself by filling in the facts on this small multiplication grid, which is part of the familiar 10 x 10 multiplication square. (You need not fill in the square numbers, because the puzzle rules do not allow you to repeat a number in any row or column.)

After completing the multiplication grid, fold it back before beginning on the puzzle.

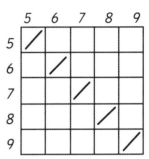

MAD Puzzle   **Digits 5 to 9**

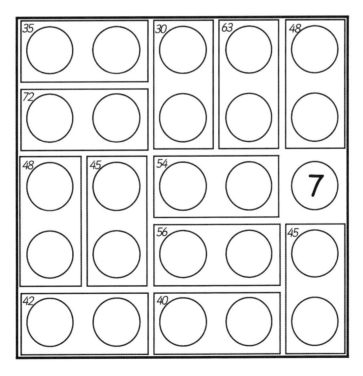

99   MAD Puzzle

Teaching points

▶ Times tables facts up to 9×9.

▶ Finding factors of given multiples.

▶ The connection between multiplication and division and between factors and products.

▶ Logical reasoning.

Note to member of staff or parent

▶ There must be no counting in ones, on fingers or otherwise.

▶ If the child attempts to chant any table from its beginning, that table needs more practice using reasoning methods to find answers from the known key tables facts.

▶ The child should use only logic. The puzzles in this book have been carefully designed so that the solver need never resort to guesswork or trial and error.

Equipment needed

A pencil and rubber.

99. MAD Puzzle

Name:

Date:

When to hand it in:

Instructions

Write the factors 3 to 9 in the circles so that each digit appears only once in each row and each column. The number shown at the top left of a rectangle enclosing two circles is the product of the two circled numbers.

MAD Puzzle   **Digits 3 to 9**

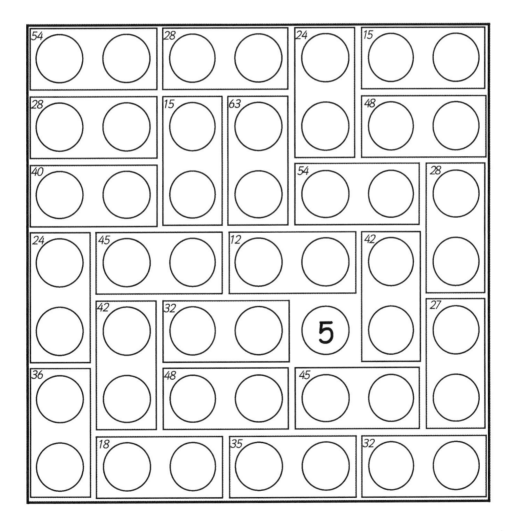

The Dyscalculia Resource Book © Ronit Bird, 2011 (SAGE)

100   R for Remainder – a game for 2 or 3 players

Teaching points

▶ Remainders in division.

▶ Practice in multiplying two numbers up to 6 × 6.

▶ Practice in dividing amounts between 1 and 36 by numbers between 1 and 6.

▶ Some of the basic divisibility rules, e.g.

any number divided by 1 remains unchanged
even numbers divided by 2 leave no remainders
odd numbers divided by 2 leave a remainder of 1
only numbers ending in 5 or 0 can be divided by 5 without leaving a remainder, etc.

Note to member of staff or parent

▶ Players should find the answer to the multiplication question before tackling the division.

▶ Encourage the children to think aloud. Make sure they are able to demonstrate that answers not known immediately are derived from key facts or from previous answers, without resorting to counting in ones.

▶ Players should be prepared to explain, if challenged, how any remainder is calculated.

▶ Allow the children to discover for themselves that if the number on the third die is a factor of one of the numbers on the other two dice, there will be no remainder.

▶ The game should be played more than once and on more than one occasion.

Equipment needed

Three ordinary dice, of which two are a matching pair and the third can be distinguished by virtue of its different size or different colour. A token for each player.

100. R for Remainder

Name:

Date:

Instructions

Take turns to throw three dice, of which two are a matching pair while the third is different in either colour or size. Multiply the numbers on the paired dice, then divide by the number on the third die. If there is no remainder, that is the end of your turn. If there is a remainder, move your token to match the amount of the remainder, i.e. move 3 spaces for a remainder of 3, etc. The winner is the first to reach or pass the end of the track.

R for Remainder

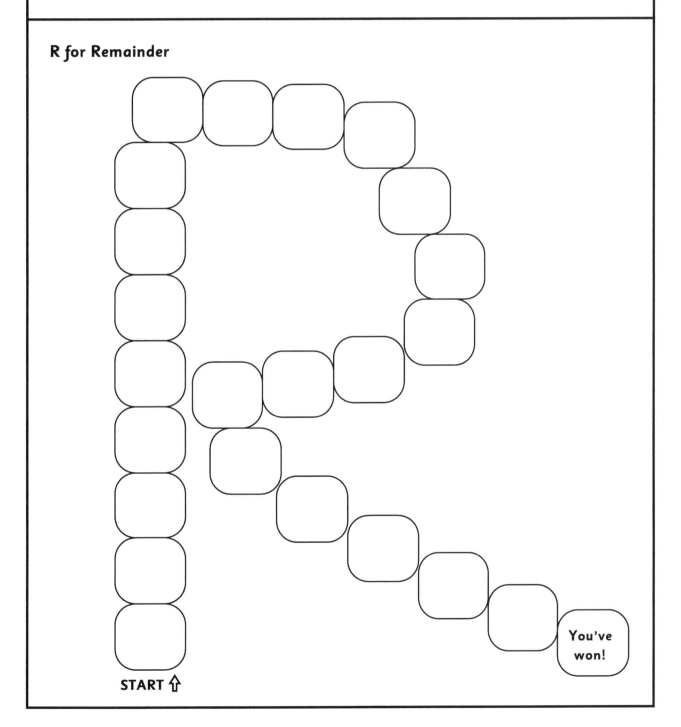

The Dyscalculia Resource Book © Ronit Bird, 2011 (SAGE)

Solutions to Su Doku Puzzles

Puzzle 9

5	2	4	1	3
4	1	3	2	5
3	4	1	5	2
1	5	2	3	4
2	3	5	4	1

Puzzle 11

3	5	1	4	2
1	2	5	3	4
2	3	4	5	1
4	1	3	2	5
5	4	2	1	3

Puzzle 13

3	1	2	5	4
2	4	5	1	3
4	3	1	2	5
1	5	3	4	2
5	2	4	3	1

Puzzle 15

3	1	5	4	2
1	5	2	3	4
4	3	1	2	5
2	4	3	5	1
5	2	4	1	3

Puzzle 17

4	2	3	5	6
3	6	5	2	4
2	5	4	6	3
6	4	2	3	5
5	3	6	4	2

Puzzle 19

2	3	4	6	5
3	4	6	5	2
5	6	2	3	4
6	2	5	4	3
4	5	3	2	6

Puzzle 21

5	4	2	3	6
2	3	4	6	5
6	2	5	4	3
3	5	6	2	4
4	6	3	5	2

Puzzle 23

5	6	3	4	2
4	2	6	3	5
3	4	2	5	6
2	5	4	6	3
6	3	5	2	4

Puzzle 26

7	5	4	6	3
3	4	6	7	5
4	7	5	3	6
5	6	3	4	7
6	3	7	5	4

Puzzle 28

5	3	4	6	7
7	4	5	3	6
3	7	6	5	4
6	5	7	4	3
4	6	3	7	5

Puzzle 30

3	6	7	5	4
5	7	3	4	6
6	4	5	3	7
4	3	6	7	5
7	5	4	6	3

Puzzle 32

5	3	4	7	6
4	6	7	3	5
6	5	3	4	7
3	7	5	6	4
7	4	6	5	3

Puzzle 34

8	5	4	6	7
4	7	6	5	8
6	8	7	4	5
5	4	8	7	6
7	6	5	8	4

Puzzle 36

7	5	4	6	8
4	7	8	5	6
8	6	7	4	5
6	4	5	8	7
5	8	6	7	4

Puzzle 38

4	7	5	6	8
7	5	4	8	6
8	4	6	7	5
5	6	8	4	7
6	8	7	5	4

Puzzle 40

8	5	4	6	7
5	4	7	8	6
4	8	6	7	5
7	6	8	5	4
6	7	5	4	8

Puzzle 41

4	3	5	2	6	1
1	2	4	6	5	3
6	5	1	3	4	2
2	4	6	1	3	5
3	6	2	5	1	4
5	1	3	4	2	6

Puzzle 42

7	5	6	9	8
6	8	9	5	7
8	7	5	6	9
5	9	7	8	6
9	6	8	7	5

Puzzle 43

3	2	5	1	4
1	5	4	3	2
5	1	2	4	3
2	4	3	5	1
4	3	1	2	5

Puzzle 44

6	8	5	9	7
8	7	9	6	5
5	9	8	7	6
9	6	7	5	8
7	5	6	8	9

Puzzle 45

3	2	7	6	5	4
6	4	5	2	3	7
2	5	6	4	7	3
4	7	3	5	6	2
7	6	2	3	4	5
5	3	4	7	2	6

Puzzle 46

6	9	8	7	5
5	7	9	8	6
8	5	7	6	9
9	8	6	5	7
7	6	5	9	8

Puzzle 47

2	4	5	1	3
5	1	3	4	2
1	3	2	5	4
3	5	4	2	1
4	2	1	3	5

Puzzle 48

9	5	8	6	7
6	7	9	5	8
5	8	7	9	6
7	6	5	8	9
8	9	6	7	5

Puzzle 49

5	4	9	8	7	6
6	7	8	5	4	9
7	8	4	6	9	5
9	6	5	4	8	7
8	5	7	9	6	4
4	9	6	7	5	8

Solutions to MAD Puzzles

Puzzle 55a

2	1	4	3
4	3	2	1
1	4	3	2
3	2	1	4

Puzzle 55b

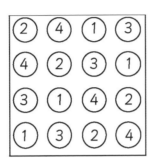

2	4	1	3
4	2	3	1
3	1	4	2
1	3	2	4

Puzzle 59a

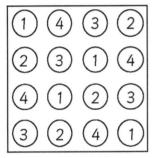

1	4	3	2
2	3	1	4
4	1	2	3
3	2	4	1

Puzzle 59b

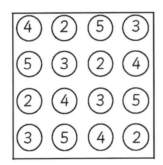

4	2	5	3
5	3	2	4
2	4	3	5
3	5	4	2

Puzzle 61

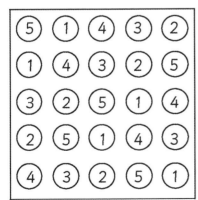

5	1	4	3	2
1	4	3	2	5
3	2	5	1	4
2	5	1	4	3
4	3	2	5	1

Puzzle 63

4	1	3	5	2
1	5	4	2	3
2	3	5	1	4
5	4	2	3	1
3	2	1	4	5

Puzzle 65

2	3	1	4	5
4	1	5	2	3
3	5	2	1	4
5	2	4	3	1

Puzzle 67

4	6	3	5	2
5	3	6	2	4
6	2	5	4	3
3	4	2	6	5

Puzzle 69

6	4	3	5	2
5	3	2	4	6
3	5	6	2	4
2	6	4	3	5
4	2	5	6	3

Puzzle 71

5	4	2	3	6
2	3	4	6	5
6	2	5	4	3
3	5	6	2	4
4	6	3	5	2

Puzzle 73

5	6	4	3	2	1
1	3	6	2	5	4
4	2	3	6	1	5
6	1	2	5	4	3

Puzzle 75

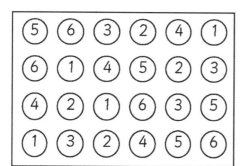

Puzzle 77

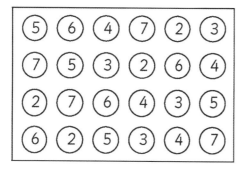

Puzzle 79

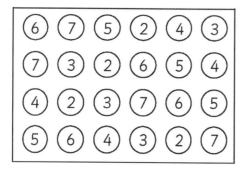

Puzzle 81

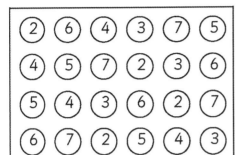

Puzzle 83

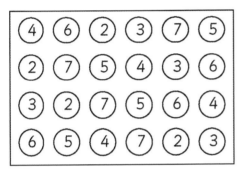

Puzzle 85

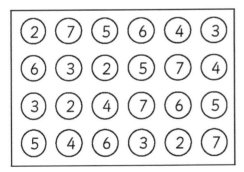

Puzzle 87

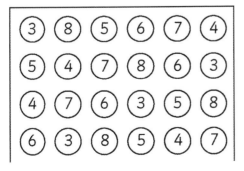

Puzzle 89

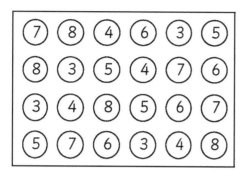

Puzzle 91

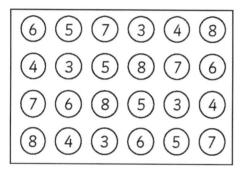

Puzzle 92

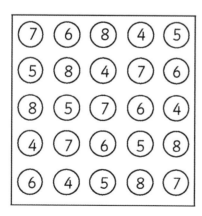

Puzzle 94

```
7  6  4  8  5
5  4  8  7  6
8  5  7  6  4
4  7  6  5  8
6  8  5  4  7
```

Puzzle 95

```
4  6  7  5  8
8  7  5  4  6
5  8  4  6  7
7  4  6  8  5
6  5  8  7  4
```

Puzzle 96

```
8  5  4  7  6
5  6  7  8  4
6  7  5  4  8
4  8  6  5  7
7  4  8  6  5
```

Puzzle 97

Puzzle 98

Puzzle 99

Appendix: DIGIT CARDS

Because it is so difficult to buy digit cards that differentiate between the 6 and the 9, here is a template for making your own cards. Enlarge as desired and laminate each page before cutting out the cards. A standard pack of digit cards is made of four of each of the digits between 1 and 9 inclusive. Zeros and/or tens are optional. The digits below are given as outlines because numbers often show through paper cards. If there is still a problem with show-through, either use brightly coloured paper and/or thicker paper or print a whole page of repeated words (e.g. 'digit cards') on the reverse of each page.

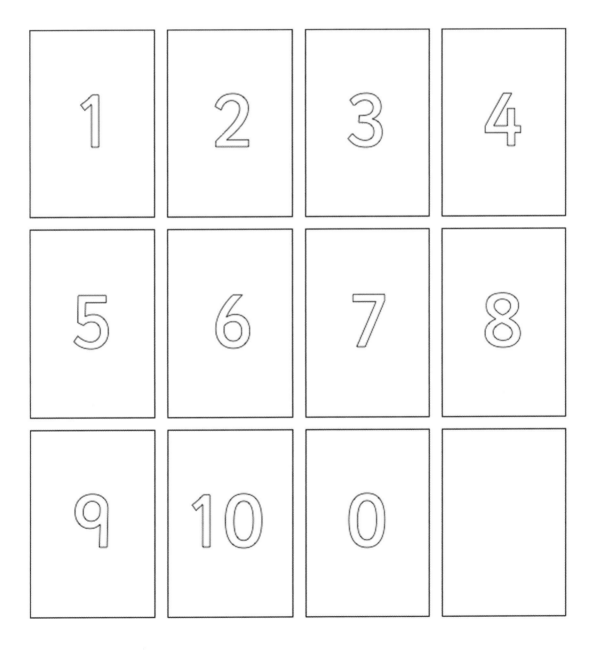

Glossary

Addend   A quantity or number that is added to another. For example, in the problem 6 + 8, both 6 and 8 are addends. In the problem 6 + ☐ = 10, the missing addend is 4.

Bridging   A technique based on a linear understanding of the number system, by which addition or subtraction is performed not in single steps but in convenient chunks or jumps. For example, to find 7 + 7 a first jump – a bridging jump – takes you from 7 to 10 (+3, in this example) and a second jump adds whatever remains (+4, in this example). Because ours is a decimal number system, it is generally 10, or a multiple of 10, that acts as a stepping stone for bridging.

Chunking   Grouping together a small number of items.

Complement   The quantity or number that completes another. In this book, it is usually 10 that is considered to be the number that needs to be completed. For example, 2 is the complement of 8, so 8 and 2 are complements to (or complements of) 10.

Component   A constituent part of a larger whole. I often use the word 'component' as a way of distinguishing between a chunking approach and a ones-based approach. For example, the components of 6 are 3 and 3, or 2 and 4, or 5 and 1, or 1 and 2 and 3. By contrast, a ones-based approach regards 6 as if it were only ever built from 1 + 1 + 1 + 1 + 1 + 1. Component facts are also known as 'number bonds'. The **key components** of any of the numbers up to 10 are the double or near double facts about the number, i.e. of all the ways of making 6 listed above, it is 3 + 3 that is considered to be the key fact, from which the other components can be derived by logic.

Commutative property   The characteristic of an operation in which the numbers can be taken in any order without altering the result. For example, addition is commutative because 3 + 5 = 5 + 3 and multiplication is commutative because 3 × 5 = 5 × 3.

Complementary addition   A method for subtraction that is based on the idea of complements, or completing a number, by working forwards to find the difference between two numbers or quantities. For example, the solution to 15 – 8 is found by bridging up from 8 through 10 and then to 15.

Concrete materials   Mathematical materials that can be physically handled and manipulated, such as counters, **nuggets**, base-10 blocks and **Cuisenaire rods**. All the games and puzzles in this book are designed to practise and reinforce in a more abstract manner what children have already been taught through concrete means. (For details of how to use concrete materials to teach and learn numeracy, please see my two previous books *The Dyscalculia Toolkit* (2007) and *Overcoming Difficulties with Number* (2009).)

Cuisenaire rods   Wooden or plastic cuboids with a cross-section measuring 1 cm square, in ten lengths starting with 1 cm and increasing by increments of 1 cm. Each length of rod has a distinctive and unvarying colour to aid recognition and to eliminate the need to count in ones in order to identify which rod represents each of the numbers between 1 and 10.

Empty number line   See **Number line**.

Factor   A number or a quantity that divides exactly into another, leaving no remainder. For example, 5 is a factor of 15. The other factors of 15 are 1, 3 and 15.

Key facts and **key component facts**   Key facts are targeted in many of my games, not because they are more important than other facts but because our decimal number system renders them easier to learn and to memorise. Those with memory difficulties can be reassured that they need to know only a small repertoire of key facts and can be taught how to use reasoning and logic to derive other numeracy facts from them. See also **Component** and **Times table**.

Multiple   A number or a quantity that can be divided exactly by another, leaving no remainder. For example, 15, 20 and 125 are all multiples of 5.

Nuggets   Small polished hemispherical pieces, often made of coloured plastic or iridescent glass and sold as vase fillers or table decorations. They make an attractive alternative to counters.

Number bond   See **Component**.

Number line   An abstract and linear model of the number system on which numbers are represented as points on the line. Not to be confused with a number track, on which a defined space, or area, is allocated to each number. The most versatile kind of number line for supporting mental arithmetic is an **empty number line**, on which no number is labelled in advance of a calculation being carried out. Addition or subtraction is represented as movement along the line and sketched above the line as arcs to illustrate component 'jumps'.

Partitioning   Splitting into separate segments or component parts. When a number is partitioned it is split into two or more smaller components. For example, 12 can be partitioned into 6 and 6, or into 10 and 2, or into 3 fours, etc.

Place value   The system in which a digit's value is determined by its place or position within a number. For example, in the number 555 each of the fives carries a different value.

Product   The number or quantity that results from multiplying two or more numbers together. For example, the product of 3 and 5 is 15.

Round number   A colloquial expression often used for any number ending in zero, otherwise known as a 'multiple of 10'.

Times table   A colloquial expression often used for the first ten multiples of a number, in order. Also known as multiplication tables, the 100 facts are particularly difficult for dyslexic and dyscalculic learners to memorise. For this reason, pupils can be encouraged to learn only the key tables facts and taught to find all the other facts by reasoning and logic. The three **key facts**

about any multiplication table are the 2×, 5× and 10× steps of the table, because these facts exhibit clear numerical patterns – ours being a decimal (base 10) number system – which makes them easy to learn.

Triad   A group of three. In this book, the word 'triad' describes an arrangement of three numbers positioned in a triangular array so that the number at the top is equal in value to the two numbers below. Triads are useful as an informal notation to support mental arithmetic because they show number relationships in terms of both addition and subtraction at the same time.

THE DYSCALCULIA TOOLKIT

Supporting Learning Difficulties in Maths

Ronit Bird *Teacher, London*

Includes CD Rom

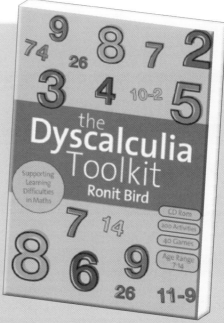

'This is an excellent resource...suitable for use with all learners between the ages of 7 and 14, but particularly for supporting pupils experiencing significant and specific difficulties in mathematics'
- **SENCO Update**

'Yes!! This book is a winner. At last someone is addressing in detail many of the challenges these students are meeting....A wonderful toolkit!'
- *Jenny Stent, SENCO, International Student Co-ordinator, Hankanui School, Hamilton, New Zealand*

'Who says numbers are boring?! This is a bright and inviting addition to any good support library...this toolkit does what it says on the packet. A ready to run resource that is very user friendly. Lots of game based activities with clear instructions. Ideas would be useful for students with specific difficulties, however the fun based element will help all students enjoy working with numbers'- *TES website*

'Finally, a book which understands! This book is full of pain-free games and activities which show that the author really gets dyscalculia. Things are broken down well so there are opportunities to build up basic understanding without getting bogged down and overwhelmed - and never a worksheet in sight. Now my daughter is happy to sit down and do maths with me. I'm really delighted with this - it has filled a real gap' - *Amazon Reviewer*

'This book is absolutely brilliant! I would highly recommend it to any parent or teacher who has a child or children with numberwork difficulties. Very easy and exciting to use' - *Amazon Reviewer*

This collection of 200 teaching activities and 40 games to use with pupils who struggle with maths is based on the author's years of experience in schools, working with dyslexic, dyspraxic and dyscalculic pupils - but all the suggested strategies are equally suitable for teaching the basics of numeracy to any pupil aged 7 to 14.

The toolkit covers:

- early number work with numbers under 10
- basic calculations with numbers above 10
- place value
- times tables, multiplication and division

The activities and games provided can be used with individuals, pairs or small groups of pupils, and the CD Rom accompanying the book contains printable and photocopiable resources.

CONTENTS

Introduction \ PART ONE: EARLY NUMBER WORK - NUMBERS UP TO 10 \ PART TWO: BASIC CALCULATION WITH NUMBERS ABOVE 10 \ PART THREE: PLACE VALUE \ PART FOUR: TIMES TABLES, MULTIPLICATION AND DIVISION

2007 • 160 pages
Cloth (978-1-4129-4764-0) • £85.00
Paper (978-1-4129-4765-7) • £32.99

ALSO FROM SAGE

OVERCOMING DIFFICULTIES WITH NUMBER

Supporting Dyscalculia and Students who Struggle with Maths

Ronit Bird *Teacher, London*

In writing this practical book, Ronit Bird has drawn on her teaching and training experience to create teaching plans for key numeracy topics, aimed at those working with students aged 9-16.

She provides detailed strategies for teaching numeracy skills through a progression of practical activities and visualisation techniques which build the self-esteem of students who need extra help and give them a basic foundation in number. While the plans cover the National Numeracy Strategy, they can also be used in any setting where maths is being taught.

Topics covered include:

- games and puzzles for learning number components
- bridging
- multiplication
- division
- reasoning strategies

A bank of accompanying resources, games, activities and Su-Doku puzzles is available on the CD included with this book.

This is an ideal resource for both class teachers and maths subject teachers, and is equally useful for teaching assistants and learning support assistants.

CONTENTS

Introduction \ PART ONE: HOW TO HELP PUPILS STOP COUNTING IN ONES \ More Than 50 Ideas to Help Pupils Stop Counting in Ones \ PART TWO: THE BRIDGING TECHNIQUE \ Pre-Skills for Learning the Bridging Technique \ Bridging through 10 \ Bridging through Multiples of 10 \ PART THREE: THE AREA MODEL OF MULTIPLICATION AND DIVISION \ Pre-Skills for the Area Model of Multiplication and Division \ The Area Model of Multiplication and Division \ Making the Transition from the Area Model to Standard Written Algorithms for Short and Long Multiplication \ Making the Transition from the Area Model to Standard Written Algorithms for Short and Long Division \ PART FOUR: REASONING STRATEGIES \ Reasoning Strategies

READERSHIP

Class teachers and maths subject teachers, teaching assistants and learning support assistants.

2009 • 168 pages
Cloth (978-1-84860-710-1) • £72.00
Paper (978-1-84860-711-8) • £24.99

ALSO FROM SAGE

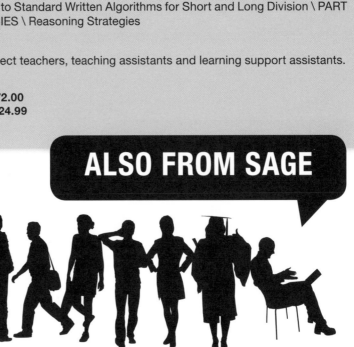